IN

ISRAEL TODAY

WITH YESHUA

A Believer's Guidebook to Israel

By
Paul & Nuala O'Higgins

"In Jerusalem My name shall be forever"
(2 Chronicles 33:4)

Walk about Zion, go round about her, number her towers, consider well her ramparts, go through her citadels; that you may tell the next generation that this is God, our God for ever and ever. He will be our guide for ever.
(Ps. 48 12-14)

In Israel Today With Yeshua
Copyright c 1987 by Paul & Nuala O'Higgins
Reconciliation Outreach Inc.,
P.O. Box 2778, Stuart, FL 34995

For world wide distribution
Published by Reconciliation Library ISBN 0-944795-01-3
First Printing 1987
Second Printing 1989
Third Printing 1995
Fourth Printing 2004

TABLE OF CONTENTS

INTRODUCTION.

A visit to Israel can be "just another tour," "just another vacation" or it can be a life changing experience.

To travel the land of Israel and to observe it in the light of the Scriptures and of present day events can electrify one's spiritual understanding of the God of the Bible.

Sadly of the millions who travel to Israel and follow the physical footsteps of Jesus, few touch the Man behind the gospel accounts, or the God behind the history of this land.

The return of the Jewish people to this land is a signal to the nations that the plan and purposes of God to "bring in everlasting peace" is advancing rapidly in our day.

This book is not a tour guide to Israel, nor is it an archaeological guide to the places where tourists visit in the land. It is a spiritual companion for all who would visit this land to explore the depths of Jesus' words, and to touch the Author of History who is guiding the destiny of the Jewish people, and the course of the nations.

Our concern is that those who read this book, or who use it as a companion to their spiritual quest in

Israel, may find themselves not only spectators of history but hear the call and promises of God as relevant to themselves. It is to us the Master calls, "Come Follow Me."

Our second concern is that the Christian reader may have his eyes open to see the hand of God at work in the regathering of the Jewish people to their ancient homeland, and may understand from this His benign call and purposes for them, and the significance of the times in which we live.

"Perhaps it is that God has YOU in the kingdom for such a time as this."

Chapter One

THE LAND OF ISRAEL — ERETZ ISRAEL AN INHERITANCE FOR ABRAHAM AND His DESCENDANTS

"And Abraham took Sarai, his wife, and Lot, his brother's son, and all their possessions which they had gathered and the persons that they had gotten in Haan; and they set forth to go to the land of Canaan. When they had come to the land of Canaan, Abram passed through the land to the place at Shechem to the oak of Moreh. At that time the Canaanites were in the land. Then the Lord appeared to Abram and said, "To your descendants I will give this land." (Gen. 12:5-7)

At the time Abram moved to this land it was already occupied by other tribes, nevertheless the Most High God, Possessor of Heaven and Earth promised Abram that his family would inherit this land, and that it would be their inheritance forever.

"After Lot had separated from Abram, the Lord confirmed His promise with him. "Lift up your eyes, and look from the place where you are, (Shechem), northward and southward and eastward and westward; for all the land, which you see I will give to

you and to your descendants FOREVER. I will make your descendants as the dust of the earth; so that if one can count the dust of the earth, your descendants also can be counted. Arise, walk through the length and breadth of the land, for I will give it to you."
(Genesis 13:14)

Ishmael And Isaac

"Now Abraham had two sons Ishmael, who was born of Hagar, the slave of his wife Sarah, and Isaac who was born of Sarah. Abraham loved both of his sons and longed to see Ishmael blessed. God said, 'As for Ishmael, I have heard you; behold I will bless him and make him fruitful and multiply him exceedingly; he shall be the father of twelve princes and I will make him a great nation. but I will establish my covenants with Isaac, whom Sarah will bear to you..." (Genesis 17:19-21)

God blessed Ishmael, who is the father of the Arab people, but Isaac was to have a special destiny and to him the promise of the land was passed. From Isaac the birthright and promises that were first given to Abraham were passed on to Jacob (Israel). *"And the Lord appeared to him (Jacob) and said, 'Do not go down to Egypt; dwell in the land of which I shall tell you. Sojourn in this land, and I will be with you, and will bless you; for to you and to your descendants I will give all these lands, and will fulfilled the oath which I wore to Abraham your father.'"* (Gen. 26:2-3)

Jacob ended his days in Egypt having gone there with his family, seventy-five people in all, to escape famine in Canaan. For four hundred years his descendants remained in exile in Egypt away from the land that the Lord had promised them. God had a time fixed for them to leave Egypt and raised up Moses to lead them Out of Egypt, and Joshua to lead them into the land of Canaan.

Their return to Canaan met with fierce opposition from the tribes that inhabited the land at the time, but God supported the Israelites in their efforts to come into their inheritance.

Canaan Lost And Canaan Regained

Moses had predicted great blessings on the tribes of Israel in this land as long as they walked uprightly before God. He also predicted dire consequences for them if they did not walk uprightly and obediently before God. *"If you are not careful to do all the words of this law which are written in this book ... then the Lord will bring upon you and your offspring extraordinary afflictions ... and you shall be plucked off the land which you are entering to take possession of it. And the Lord will scatter you among all peoples, from one end of the earth to the other...*

And among these nations you shall find no ease, and there shall be no rest for the soles of your feet; but the Lord will give you there a trembling heart, and failing eyes and a languishing soul."

Sadly, after they had conquered the land most of the peopled did not follow the Lord closely, and in 721 B.C. (500 years after they had entered the land of Canaan) the territory of the northern ten tribes was overrun by the Assyrians and the Israelites were dispossessed of their land and scattered throughout the nation.

The southern kingdom, the area of Judah and Benjamin survived nearly one hundred and fifty years more until it too fell and the people were deported to Babylon. The exile in Babylon lasted seventy years, after which a partial restoration of the nation took place. There was no radical repentance on a national scale, however, and they languished in their homeland oppressed by the different imperial powers that dominated the eastern Mediterranean. In the year 70 A. D., 40 years after the Ascension of Jesus, the city of Jerusalem was once again destroyed. This time it was by the ruthless force of the Romans. Once again the Jewish people were scattered throughout the earth, so that to this day their presence is found in the remotest parts of the world.

The prophets, from Amos all the way to Jesus, had the unenviable task of reminding the people that the consequences of disobedience that Moses had warned of would actually happen. They were not totally prophets of doom, however, for they had also another message for the tribes of Israel, a message of comfort, hope and restoration, a message promising them that God would one day gather them back to this land of promise and restore them spiritually and politically.

"Behold, I will open your graves and raise you from your graves, 0 my people; and I will bring you home into the land of Israel. And you shall know that I am the Lord, when I open your graves and raise you from your graves, O My people. And I will put my Spirit within you, and you shall live, and I will place you in your own land; then you shall know that I, the Lord, have spoken, and I have done it says the Lord."

"Behold I will take the people of Israel from the nations among whom they have gone, and will gather them from all sides, and bring them to their own land, upon the mountains of Israel; and one king shall be king over them all.; and they shall be no longer two nations, and no longer divided into two kingdoms... My servant David shall be king over them, and they shall all have one shepherd. They shall follow my ordinances and be careful to observe my statutes."
(Ezekiel: 37:12 -14, 21-22 & 24)

"I will restore the fortunes of my people Israel, and they shall rebuild the mined cities and inhabit

them; they shall plant vineyards and drink their wine, and they shall make gardens and eat their fruit. "I will plant them upon their land, and they shall never again be plucked up out of the land which I have given them," says the Lord your God.' (Amos 9:14-15)

*"And Jerusalem will be trodden down by the Gentiles, **until** the times of the Gentiles are fulfilled."* *(Luke 21:24)*

Yes the prophets foretold disasters that were to come on the people and the land of Israel, but they also foretold their eventual restoration to the land.

"Fear not, for I am with you; I will bring your offspring from the east, and from the west I will gather you. I will say to the north, 'Give up,' and to the south, 'Do not withhold; bring my sons from afar and my daughters from the end of the earth, everyone who is called by name whom I created. for my glory, whom I formed and made.'" (Is. 43:5-7)

The land of Israel is the everlasting inheritance of the descendants of Israel. It is the possession that they lost because of their own disobedience and the hostility of other nations. In this century we have witnessed the faithfulness of God to keep His promise to His people to bring them back to their land. In spite of the atrocities committed against the Jewish people He has established them back in their land. As He promised, these prophecies of restoration have to be fulfilled if God's word is to be believed. Some may argue that God fulfilled these promises of restoration when He brought them back from Babylon. To this we answer, "How can their return from Babylon in 538 B.C. fulfill prophecies spoken by Jesus and Zephaniah and others who spoke AFTER that return from Babylon?" Also the return from Babylon consisted only of a return from ONE country and from one direction, and does not fulfill what the prophets looked for: return from ALL the nations and a return from the north, the south, the east and the west, nor does it fulfill the promise that they would never again be uprooted from the land.

"At that time I will bring you home, at that time when I gather you together; yea I will make you renowned and praise among all the peoples of the earth, when I restore your fortunes before your eyes, says the Lord." (Zeph: 3:20)

The present day Jewish people's return to the land of Israel is the fulfillment of God's ancient promises, and the predictions of the prophets. From this amazing miracle of their restoration, we know that we are in the days when they will receive a new heart and rejoice in the rule of a new king David over them. God said that they would be brought back and that afterwards He would pour clean water upon them, and put His spirit within them. A tremendous spiritual restoration will take place among this people, before the Messiah returns to take possession of the throne of David.

Ezekiel predicted (Ezekiel 38) that after the Jewish people return to Israel they will be attacked by an alliance from Russia, Iran and Libya. No doubt fierce anti-Semitism will motivate these allies. Their hostile efforts will not succeed, however, and will result in their humiliation and defeat. The winds of this hostility are blowing in the Middle East today.

Arab And Jewish People In The Land Of Israel

In the past relations between Arab and Jew in Israel have been cordial, bound together by a common solidarity of being politically dominated by an outside power. From 1517 until 1918 the area of Palestine was a neglected possession of the Ottoman Turkish Empire. At first Jewish immigration to the land was welcomed by the Arabs of Palestine and the neighboring countries, but when it became clear that the Jewish people intended to establish a nation there this was resisted by the Muslim Arabs. About twelve percent of the Arabs of the land of Israel are Christian

The native Palestinian Arabs have never had sovereignty over the land. The resentment of some Palestinians to the state of Israel has been exploited by some neighboring Arab states, which cannot tolerate the existence of this new non-Muslim state in the Middle East. In fact Palestinian nationalism did not exist until the State of Israel was created. It has emerged as a reaction against the establishment of Israel.

Anti-Israel sentiment among Moslems is a smoldering fire that is being fueled by anti-Zionist propaganda. (A Zionist is a person that believes that the Jewish people have a right to the land that was promised them by God forever.) Today's anti-Zionism is no different than the anti-Semitism that swept through central Europe during the 1930's and 1940's and which has manifested repeatedly against the Jewish people. Palestinian Arabs' rights and culture must be respected and some legitimate grievances may have to be rectified, but present day anti-Semitism and anti-Zionism cannot be condoned by anyone who loves God, respects His word and the sovereignty He holds over the nations of the world.

To Abraham, God said, *"I will bless those who bless you, and him who curses you I will curse; and in you all the families of the earth will be blessed."* (Genesis 12:3)

For the Arab people, God has promised special blessings. He does not love the Israelis any more than He loves the Arabs, but He has placed a special call on the descendants of Abraham, Isaac, and Jacob. To oppose that call is to set oneself against the purposes of God. The hostility of the Arab nations against Israel has put the nation on a constant state of defensiveness. The exploitation of the Arab people by anti-Semitic extremists is a threat not only to Israeli interests but to Arab interests as well. God is not against the Arabs, He is for them. He is against anti-Semitism wherever it manifests.

Pray for the Peace of Jerusalem and the welfare of all its citizens, Jew, Arab and Christian.

Chapter Two

THE CITY OF JERUSALEM

When the people of Israel came into the land of Canaan, in the days of Joshua, a Canaanite tribe, the Jebusites, inhabited the city of Jerusalem. It was known as the Jebusite city, and was not captured by the people of Israel until the days of King David c. 1000 B.C. (1 Chronicles 11:4-7) When he became king, David established the city as the headquarters of his dynasty, and reinforced this by bringing the Ark of the Covenant to the city. Thus he made Jerusalem the political and spiritual focus of the nation.

After David's death, Solomon built the first temple. This was a center and symbol of God's rule over the people and the place where the tribes came three times each year to celebrate the feasts prescribed by the Lord. From Dan to Beersheba each Passover, Shavuot (Pentecost) and Tabernacles the people came by mule and on foot, thronging to this city where God dwelt. It was here that the bond of unity between the tribes was maintained as they came together under common unity to the one true God, who, though He inhabits the heavens is pleased to dwell with men. The ancient world was filled with temples. From the furthest regions of Cathay to the deepest forest of Africa, from Gaul to Babylon there were temples ... all expressions of man's acknowledgment of spiritual forces that shape and guide his destiny. To only one people God had revealed himself as YHWH the One who is, who was and who is to come. The One bigger than temples made by human hands, and yet who had chosen to reveal Himself to this people of Israel so that the world could learn to walk with Him.

God had promised to keep them in security in this land if they continued to acknowledge Him as their source of blessing and to walk in His ways. He warned them that if they did not stay close to Him they would be overcome by the nations around them. (Dt. 28:36-37, 47-50)

In the days after Solomon, the kingdom was tragically divided, and most people did not come up to Jerusalem to the Temple for the feasts anymore. Instead they reverted to Canaanite superstitions and idol worship. The Spirit of God stirred the prophets to speak out against these vile practices but without success. Finally the prophets realized that the people of Israel and Judah had gone too far away from God and His standards. They predicted that He would allow them to be uprooted from the land just as He had warned through Moses.

Jeremiah c. 600 B.C. prophesied that Jerusalem was about to fall, that the people would be deported to Babylon and be held there for 70 years. Then they would return to their homeland. He foretold the scattering of the people from Jerusalem and their eventual return to that city. His words were fulfilled to the letter. The city was taken and destroyed by King Nebuchadnezzar of Babylon in the year 587, and was left depopulated until the end of the sixth century. In 539 King Cyrus of Persia overthrew the Babylonians and under him and his successors, the Jewish people were permitted to resettle in their homeland and to rebuild the city of Jerusalem and its temple. The work went on under the governor Zerubbabel, Ezra and Nehemiah. This temple stood until 70 A.D. It was refurbished and enlarged in the reign of King Herod in a project that he instigated in the year 19 B. C.

The years of the second temple from the days of Ezra and Nehemiah to 70 A. D. were difficult, and inglorious for the people of Israel. During that time Jerusalem became first a part of the Ptolemaic Hellenic Empire, administered from Alexandria, Egypt. Then it became a part of the Seleucid Hellenic Empire, which was administered from Antioch. Then in the first century B.C. it came fell to the Romans.

By the time of the birth of Jesus the Romans had effectively crushed the power of the Jewish resistance. There was a great longing among the people for a Messiah who would relieve them of the heavy burden of Rome. The priesthood, however, had compromised heavily with the Roman authorities, and religious and political life in Israel was at an extremely low point.

In the spirit of Jeremiah and Ezekiel before him, Jesus in his role as a prophet predicted that the backslidden state of the people would result in another forfeiture of the city of Jerusalem and their land. The woeful predictions of Moses would once again be fulfilled. The people would once again be uprooted because they had not walked in submission and obedience to God. (Luke 13:34-35; 21-24) Like Jeremiah, Jesus wept over Jerusalem, and like Jeremiah his prophecy of destruction and deportation infuriated many of the religious leaders to the point where they conspired to kill him. The Romans, fearing His kingdom would be a threat to their rule, carried out His execution.

In 70 A. D., less than 40 years after Jesus' death and resurrection, the Roman army under Titus Flavius, besieged and subsequently destroyed both the city of Jerusalem and the temple. This was in fulfillment of the words of Moses in Deuteronomy 28, and in fulfillment of the unwelcome prophecies of Jesus.

Jesus had said: *"But when you see Jerusalem surrounded by armies, then know that its desolation has come near. Then let those who are inside the city depart, and let not those who are out in the country enter it; for these are days of vengeance to fulfill all that is written. Alas for those who are with child and for those who give suck in those days! For great distress shall be upon the earth and wrath upon this people; they will fall by the edge of the sword and be led captive among all nations; and Jerusalem will be trodden down by the gentiles, until the times of the gentiles are fulfilled.*(Luke 19:20-24)

Daniel, too, had prophesied that Jerusalem would be desolate again. However, as Jeremiah the prophet of the first desolation of Jerusalem, saw that its desolation would not be permanent but that eventually the Jewish people would take possession of the city again, so too Jesus foretold that the domination of the city of Jerusalem by the Gentiles would not be permanent and that eventually the Jewish people would take possession and control of the city again. "Jerusalem will be trodden down by the Gentiles, UNTIL (i.e., not forever) the times of the Gentiles are fulfilled.'

In 1967 after 1900 years of Gentile domination, the city of Jerusalem came back into Jewish hands. This prophecy of Jesus was fulfilled. We can say therefore that 1967 marks the end of "the times of the Gentiles," for in that year the domination of the city of Jerusalem by Gentile nations expired.

1967 marks a great turning point in God's timetable for humanity. Although He inhabits eternity, God is keeping a definite timetable in His plan for the fullness of time to "reconcile to himself all things." (Colossians 1:20)

"Immediately after the tribulation of those days (i.e., the Gentile domination of Jerusalem), 'the sun will be darkened and the moon will not give its light, and the stars will fall from heaven, and the powers of the heavens will be shaken; then will appear the sign of the Son of man in the heaven, and then all the tribes of the earth will mourn, and they will sec the sign of the Son of man coming in the clouds of heaven with power and great glory; and he will send out his angels with a loud trumpet call and they will gather his elect from the four winds, from one end of heaven to the other."

"From the fig tree learn its lesson: as soon as its branch becomes tender and puts forth its leaves, you know that summer is near. So also when you see all these thing you know that He is near at the very gates. Truly, I say to you this generation (the generation that witnesses the end of Gentile domination over Jerusalem) will not pass away till all these things take place."(Matthew 24:29-34)

From the sign of the return of Jerusalem to Jewish hands we can safely say that we are now living in the count down days to the return the Messiah and the establishment of His kingdom on earth.

Jerusalem Is The Key.

As we observe the signs of the times we can be alert to what God is unfolding in the history of our day and also perhaps may have the privilege of being that generation of believers who will be *"alive and remain until the coming of the Lord."*

When Jesus does return to the earth the Jewish people will recognize Him as their glorious Messiah. His feet will touch the Mount of Olives and He will establish His rule from this amazing city, the city of the Great King. God's promise to David will be fulfilled in this city: *"And when thy days be fulfilled, and you shall sleep with your fathers, I will set up thy seed after you who shall proceed out of thy bowels, and I will establish His kingdom ... And your house and your kingdom shall be established forever before you. Your throne shall be established forever.* (2 Sam 7:12-16)

The hopes of Christians and Jewish people throughout the world are merging in a common hope for the coming of the Messiah. This period however, is not to be a period of passive waiting and speculation about the future, but it is a period in which the Holy Spirit is actively preparing a company from every tribe and tongue and people and. nation who will reign with

Jesus at His coming. Will you be among those who will form that bridal party, or will you be with those who are not alert to the signs of his coming?

"Hallelujah! For the Lord our God the Almighty reigns. Let us rejoice and exalt and give him the glory, for the marriage of the Lamb has come, and His bride has made herself ready." (Rev. 19:7)

Are you getting yourself ready?

Struggle For Jerusalem

The prophet Zechariah predicted the present day international struggle over Jerusalem nearly 2500 years ago. He saw that before the Messiah returns there will be much contention between the nations over Jerusalem. This contention will culminate in their recognizing their Messiah.

"Behold, I am going to make Jerusalem a cup that causes reeling to all the people round about. I will make Jerusalem a heavy stone for all the peoples, all who lift it will be severely injured. And all the nations of the earth will be gathered against it. In that day the Lord will defend the inhabitants of Jerusalem and will set about to destroy all the nations who come against her. I will pour out upon the house of David the Spirit of grace and of supplications, so they will look upon Me whom they have pierced and will mourn for Him as one mourns for an only son." (Zechariah 12:2 - 10)

Chapter Three

PRAY FOR THE PEACE OF JERUSALEM

*'I was glad when they said to me, "Let us go to
the house of the Lord!"
Our feet have been standing within your gates, O
Jerusalem!
Jerusalem, built as a city which is bound firmly
together, to which the tribes go up, the tribes of the
Lord, as was decreed for Israel to give thanks to the
name of the Lord. Their thrones for judgment were set,
the thrones of the house of David.
PRAY FOR The PEACE OF JERUSALEM!
"May they prosper who love you!
Peace be within your walls, and security within your
towers!
For my brethren. and companion's sake I will say,
'Peace be within you!'
For the sake of the house of the Lord our God,
I will seek your good."* (Psalm 122)
*"Comfort., comfort my people says your God
Speak tenderly to Jerusalem, and cry to her that her
time of service is ended that her iniquity is pardoned,
that she has received from the Lord's hand double for
all her sins.   "A voice cries In the wilderness prepare*

the way of the Lord, make straight in the desert a highway for our God. Every valley shall be lifted up, and every mountain and hill laid low; the uneven ground shall become level, and the rough places a plain. And the glory of the Lord shall be revealed.'" (Is. 40:1-5)

"Upon your wall', O Jerusalem, I have set watchmen; all the day and all the night they shall never be silent. You who put the Lord in remembrance, take no rest, and give him no rest until he establishes Jerusalem and makes it a praise in the earth." (Is. 62:6-7)

Since the days of David's Jerusalem, the City of Peace has had little real peace. Situated at the crossroads between Europe, Asia and Africa it has been snared and in a tug of war between surrounding nations and empires for the last 3000 years. When peace will come to Jerusalem the nations of the world will be at peace with one another.

Today the city is the capital of Israel, and the Jewish people, long a wandering nation, have a homeland and control of their capital city again. Side by side with them in the city of Jerusalem live the Moslem and Christian Arabs. These Arab families have watched the city come under the control of many succeeding peoples since the Jewish people were dispersed in 70 A.D. The Romans were displaced by the Byzantine Christians (325 A.D.) Moslems overcame the Christians in 638 A.D., until the Latin Christian Crusaders captured the city in 1099 A.D. and made Jerusalem the capital of the Latin Kingdom. In 1187 the Moslems under Saladin the Great captured the city. From 1517 until 1917 the land of Israel and the city of Jerusalem languished under Turkish rule.

In 1917 during World War I, the Turkish Empire collapsed and the British administered the land until their withdrawal in 1948. With the sanction of the United Nations the Jewish people (many of them arriving from the horror of the Holocaust) set up the modem state of Israel.

As the Jewish people proclaimed the nation of Israel, they knew they would face resistance from the Arabs in the region. War broke out in 1948, 1967 and 1973 between the infant Jewish state and the neighboring Arabs. The Jewish people instigated none of these wars. Though many Arabs are willing to live in peace with Israel and appreciate the democratic freedoms there, the political peace of Jerusalem is fragile Roused up by militant Islamic jihadists the Israeli people face danger from invasion, from suicide bomber and terrorists on a daily basis.

As discouraging as this is the sympathy of many nations to those who hate them is even more discouraging.

The nation of Israel is the only non-Arab nation in the huge subcontinent, the Middle East. Yet what the Arab people fail to recognize is that these people have been promised this land since God spoke to Abraham. The prophets foretold that they would be uprooted and would be restored one day to their land. Moslems believe that God has withdrawn His promises to Israel and the land belongs to Islam. Arab hostility to the Jewish people is grounded not only on a failure to recognize the Jewish people's divine mandate to occupy this land, but also in the agenda of Islam, to politically dominate the Middle East and eventually the whole world. Anti-Israel terrorism is rooted not only in issues of social justice and nationalism but is grounded on the spiritual agenda of fanatic Islam that is willing to use terrorism as a tool of Jihad.

All who believe in the God of the Bible must recognize the miracle of modern Israel and see in it the fulfillment of these great prophecies.

"Behold I will take the people from the nations among which they have gone and will gather them from all sides, and bring them to their own land, upon the mountains of Israel" (Ezekiel 37:21-22)

The fact that God has promised and given this land to the physical descendants of Abraham, Isaac and Jacob does not mean that He loves the Arab people any less. His promise is to bless all nations and his salvation is for Jews and Gentile without distinction.

The call to occupy this land, and rule in it, and live in it in a godly way is given to the Jewish people. In LOVE there is no distinction between Jew and Arab. In CALL there is.

Christians, who acknowledge the hand of God in the return of the Jewish people to Israel and in the birthing of the state, cannot support any policy that would deny to the Jewish people this uniquely God-given right. On the other hand recognition of the place of the Jewish people must go hand in hand with a love and respect of the Arab peoples. Many Jewish people and Arabs live in good relationships with each other. Some Arabs have become victims of anti-Jewish ideology but this is not true of all Arabs in the region. Christian Arabs who make up about 12% of the Arabs in Israel are often politically neutral. We pray

> ❖ that the love of God will touch the hearts of Jew, Arab and Christians;
> ❖ that more and more Arabs will recognize the Jewish right to inhabit and rule their ancient homeland;
> ❖ that the Jewish people themselves will have faith in the promises God gave them.
> ❖ Pray that Christians will be strong in standing against anti-Semitism and have the discernment to recognize the agenda of fanatic Islam.

When will peace come to this restless city called to be the city of peace? Ezekiel prophecies: *"Behold I will take the people from the nations among which they have gone, and will gather them from all sides and bring them to their own land; and I will make them one nation in the land, upon the mountains of Israel; and one king shall be king over them all and they shall be no longer two nations... My servant David shall be king over then and they shall all have one shepherd."* (Ezekiel 37:24)

The king is coming and when He comes, there will no longer be two rival nations vying for the land, but all will walk in unity under His government.

A Prayer

Heavenly Father, we pray for the peace and well being of Jerusalem and its entire people. We pray that every Jew, Arab, and Christian living in this city may come know You, as you really are. Send forth Your Spirit on this city in a special way; protect its people; give wisdom to its leaders; shed your peace into the hearts of all who live here. Let Your Name be glorified and Your purpose for Israel be protected from every evil plot. May. Set us free from ideology, and tradition that is incompatible with Your word and Your way and Your plan for your people Israel and for Jerusalem.

Chapter Four

EIN KAREM, BIRTH PLACE OF
JOHN THE BAPTIST

"In those days Mary arose and went with haste into the hill country, to a city of Judah (Fin Karem) and she entered the house of Zechariah and greeted Elizabeth. And when Elizabeth heard the greeting of Mary, the babe leaped in her womb; and Elizabeth was filled with the Holy Spirit and she exclaimed with a loud cry, 'Blessed are you among women, and blessed is the fruit of your womb! And why is this granted me, that the mother of my Lord should come tome?.. .And blessed is she who believed that there would be a fulfillment of what was spoken to her from the Lord.'

And Mary said, 'My soul magnifies the Lord.'
and my spirit rejoices in God my Savior,
for he has regarded the low estate of his handmaiden.
For behold all generations will call me blessed;
for he who is mighty has done great things for me,
and holy is his name.

And his mercy is on those who fear him from generation to generation.
He has shown strength with his arm He has scattered the proud... he has put down the mighty...
and exalted those of low degree...
He has filled the hungry with good things, and the rich he has sent empty away.
He has helped his servant Israel, in remembrance of his mercy, as he spoke to our fathers, to Abraham and his posterity forever
And Mary remained with her about three months and returned to her home.' (Luke 1:39-56)

What joy echoed through the town of Ein Karem on this happy day when Elizabeth and her cousin Mary met. Both women were pregnant through the miraculous intervention of God - the older woman pregnant with the child who would prepare the hearts of the people of Israel to receive their long awaited Messiah; the younger woman pregnant with the Messiah himself, one who had been conceived in the fullness of time.

How close is the fellowship between these women separated from each other by age and by the over sixty-mile distance between Nazareth and Ein Karem. All distance and natural differences an~ spanned by their common experience of the merciful intervention of God into their lives. Between Mary and Elizabeth there is a special "chemistry" which goes beyond kinship and natural friendship. It is the fellowship of the Holy Spirit. They understand each other in a special way because each has experienced person.. ally the intervention of God in their lives.

You and I may have many friends, acquaintances and relatives but there is no friendship to compare with the fellowship of those whose lives have been touched in similar ways by God. Even among God's people there is a special friendship that is immediately felt among those who share a similar revelation and experience of God.

Elizabeth says of Mary that *"all generations would call her blessed" and that she was blessed because "she believed that there would be a fulfillment of what was spoken to her from the Lord."*

The blessing of God that came into her life was a result of God's direct intervention in her life. We say: 'How wonderful that God blessed Mary.' She however says that God's mercy is on those who fear Him from generation to generation. In other words God wants people of every generation to receive His mercy. He wants to intervene in the life of ALL who call Him in every generation. Mary heard the word of God and she believed what was spoken to her and then God acted to fulfill the word he had spoken over her life.

God has a special plan for your life. He wants to bless you mightily and do great things for you. He awaits your response of faith so that He can fulfill His word in your life too. Our part is to believe and to lock our wills in with the revealed will of God, and it is God's part to act. God is the great agent in history and wishes to involve Himself in the lives of all who turn to Him and call on Him. He opposes the proud and self-sufficient and helps those who reach out for His help and intervention.

Mary and Elizabeth were two Israeli women who longed for God to fulfill His Messianic promises for His people and for the World. They rejoiced that God was fulfilling His plan for Israel in sending a Messiah who would be Shepherd King and Messiah.

Mary attributed her blessing to the greatness and goodness of God: *'He who is mighty has done great things for me and holy is his name.'* So often among God's people when we see someone blessed and used by God, as Mary was, we attribute to the person rather than to God that which God performs through that person. Even men of God can fall for such flattery and take credit for what God does through them. God will use us and bless us but if He does the work He must get the credit. How often we rob God by attributing to ourselves that which God does through us. How different Mary was. With overflowing thanks and praise she gave all the credit to God for the great things He has done. By praising and thanking God she did not steal the glory. She shows us that we respond best to Him

(1) by receiving His word;

(2) by believing He would perform His word;

(3) by being utterly dependent on the present day intervention of God and

(4) by praising and thanking God and thereby giving Him all the credit for what He does.

Are you learning to expect God to act in your own life? Do you believe that He will fulfill his promises for your life? Do you depend on the merciful interventions of God in your life? Do you. give Him full credit, praise, and thanks for all He has done, is doing. and will do in our lives?

A Prayer

Lord, invade every part of my life with Your fulfilling mercies. Show me how I can be used to advance Your plan for Your kingdom. I praise You for sending a Savior, for remembering Your promises, for blessing me and I ask you to make me more and more fruitful to You. Thank You for Mary's example and for her spirit of praise. Let me glorify You too.

Chapter Five

BETHLEHEM, BIRTHPLACE OF JESUS

"And Joseph also went up from Galilee, from the city of Nazareth, to Judea, to the city of David, which is called Bethlehem, because he was of the house and lineage of David, to be enrolled with Mary, his betrothed, who was with child. And while they were there, the time came for her to be delivered. And she gave birth to her first born son and wrapped Him in swaddling cloths, and laid Him in a manger, because there was no place for them in the inn.

And in that region there, were shepherds out in the field, keeping watch over their flock by night. And an angel of the Lord appeared to them, and the glory of the Lord shone around them, and they were filled with fear. And the angel said to them, 'Be not afraid; for behold, I bring you good news for a great joy which will come to all the people; for to you is born this day in the city of David a Savior who is Christ (Messiah) the Lord. And this will be a sign for you: You will find a babe wrapped in swaddling cloths and lying in a manger. And suddenly there was with the angel a multitude of the heavenly host praising God and saying, 'Glory to God in the highest and on earth peace goodwill among men.' (Luke 2:4-14)

"And the Word became flesh and dwelt among us, full of grace and truth; we have beheld His glory, glory as of the only Son from the Father. And from His fullness have we all received, grace upon grace. For the law was given through Moses; grace and truth came through Jesus Christ. No one has ever seen God; the only son, who is in the bosom of the Father, He has made Him known." (John 1:14 16-18)

"I have made a covenant with my chosen one, I have sworn to David my servant: I will establish your seed forever, and build up your throne to all generations." (Ps. 89:3-4)

"But you, O Bethlehem, Ephrathah, who are little to be among the clans of Judah, from you shall come forth for me one who is to be ruler in Israel, whose origin is from of old from ancient days." (Micah 5:2-3)

Most scholars now believe that the birth of Jesus probably took place either in May at the time of Shavuot (Pentecost) or in September at the time of the Feast of Tabernacles. In the winter time shepherds would not be in their fields taking care of their flocks. The present date for the celebration of Christmas comes from the era of Constantine when the pagan winter festival was replaced by Christmas.

Whatever the actual date of Jesus' birth each Christmas the eyes of the world focus on this little town, and the whole world is reminded of this "news of great joy." The Church of the Nativity marks the traditional site where Jesus was born, and is built over a cave. A little outside the town one can visit several caves, any one of which could have been the cave that protected the holy family. Here our imaginations bridge the gap of time and we too like the shepherds can pay homage to the King.

It may seem that they were victims of inhospitality when there was no room for them in the inn, but God had prepared a more simple, yet glorious place from which they could see the sky and behold the joy that rang out in heaven that night. Disappointment is often used by God to move us on to the place that He has prepared for us.

God was giving His Son to be the Lamb, the Sin Bearer of the guilt of the world, and the Shepherd who would guide all that would hear his voice. Jesus was born among the sheep in the town of bread, because He was to be the Lamb and the Bread of life. God has not left us to flounder in our darkness and confusion but was becoming involved in a total way with our history and our problems.

Jesus is the first of a new species of human beings; He is the new Adam, the second Adam, and Son of God with the nature of God in human nature.

He takes on Himself the judgments that stood against the old Adam. He has come to be the first of many, many brothers who will know God as Father. What Jesus was by nature, Son of God, He has come to make us by grace and by adoption. He has come to bring humanity into a family relationship with God.

Jesus said of Himself, I have come from heaven, not to do my own will but the will of Him who sent me.' (John 6:30) He lifts His followers into the same heavenly relationship and asks us to go from there into the entire world, into the place where ordinary people like the shepherds gather. Yet as Jesus emptied himself and came to the lowliest place He brought the presence of heaven with Him, and He asks us to do the same. Let us go from heaven into ordinary life carrying the presence of heaven with us.

Bethlehem is forever a marker that God became involved at a particular moment in history, in a particular humble location in our lives and history. He is giving us more than a law or a philosophy; He is coming to be our rescuer and Redeemer.

A Prayer

Lord, thank you for coming into our world to save, lead, and guide us. I make room in my life for you. Live in my heart, and shine your light into my life.

Chapter Six

NAZARETH, THE HOMETOWN OF JESUS

Mary Of Nazareth

"In the sixth month the angel Gabriel was sent from God to a city of Galilee named Nazareth, to a virgin betrothed to a man whose name was Joseph. And he came to her and said, 'Hail oh favored one, the Lord is with you.' But she was greatly troubled at the saying, and considered in her mind what sort of greeting this might be. And the angel said to her, 'Do not be afraid, Mary, for you have found favor with God. And behold you will conceive in your womb and bear a son, and you shall call his name Jesus. He will be great and will be called the Son of the Most High; and the Lord God will give to him the throne of his father David, and He will reign over the house of Jacob forever; and of His kingdom there will be no end.' And Mary said to the angel, 'How shall this be, since I have no husband?' And the angel said to her, 'The Holy Spirit will came upon you, and the power of the Most High will overshadow you; therefore the child to be born will be called holy, the Son of God. And behold your kinswoman, Elizabeth, in her old age

has also conceived a son; and this is the sixth month with her who was called barren, for with God nothing will be impossible.' And Mary said, 'behold, I am the handmaid of the lord; let it be to me according to your word.' And the angel departed from her." (Lk 1:26-38)

"And when they had performed everything according to the law of the Lord, they returned into Galilee to their own city Nazareth. And the child grew and became strong, filled with wisdom; and the favor of God was upon Him." (Luke 2:39-41)

Here in Nazareth Mary received her amazing call. An angel from the Lord revealed her destiny to her. God wanted to bring something wonderful to pass through her, but her consent was needed. "Let it be done," she said.

How wonderful the partnership between God and man! His plan plus our consent, plus the overshadowing of the Holy Spirit, and the power of the Most High brings His purposes to pass. God wills not by-pass our will. He needs our co-operation.

As we study God's word and listen to His voice we begin discover what He wants to bring into our lives. We can learn from Mary, whom "all generations will call blessed" and who was blessed because she believed that God would fulfill His word for her. *"Blessed is she who believe there would be a*

fulfillment of those things spoken to her by the Lord"
(Luke 1:45)

When we say, "Yes" to God's promises and plans He can fulfill them in our lives. He who did great things for Mary can do great things for us as well.

Note that Mary did not go out and do a work FOR God - she allowed God to do His work in her, with her and through her and accepted the cost of this call. As we yield ourselves to those works and destinies God has called us to, He will do great things for us too. God will bring His plans and His projects for those who are willing to abandon their own

Jesus Of Nazareth

Most of Jesus' life on earth was spent in this town of Nazareth. We know these years as the hidden years of Jesus. He lived with Mary and Joseph and in union with His Father attending His local synagogue, living as an observant Jew and studying the scriptures and the promises of God's word, and working as a carpenter. He is Emmanuel, God with us as one of us. He was content to be obscure and to learn the lessons of faithfulness, patience and simplicity until the hour came for the Father to send Him to His ministry.

"And Jesus returned in the power of the Spirit into Galilee, and a report concerning Him went out through all the surrounding country. And He taught in

their synagogues being glorified by all. And He came to Nazareth where he had been brought up; and he went to the synagogue, as His custom was, on the Sabbath day. And he stood up to read, and there was given to Him the book of the prophet Isaiah. He opened the book and found the place where it was written, 'The Spirit of the Lord is upon me, because He has anointed me to preach good news to the poor. He has sent me to proclaim release to the captives and recovering of sight to the blind, to set at liberty those who are oppressed, to proclaim the acceptable year of the Lord.' And he closed the book, and gave it back to the attendant, and sat down; and the eyes of all the synagogue were fixed on him. And He began to say to them, 'Today this scripture has been fulfilled in your hearing.' And all spoke well of Him, and wondered at the gracious words which proceeded out of his mouth; and they said, 'Is not this Joseph's son?' And he said to them, 'Doubtless you will quote to me this proverb, Physician, heal thyself; what we have heard you did at Capernaum, do here also in your own country. And he said, 'Truly, I say to you, no prophet is acceptable in his own country. But in truth, I tell you there were many widows in Israel in the days of Elijah, when the heaven was shut up three years and six months, when there came a great famine over the land; and Elijah was sent to none of them but only to Zarephath in the land of Sidon, to a woman who was a widow. And there were many lepers in Israel in the time of the prophet Elijah; and none of them were cleansed, but only Naaman the Syrian.' When they heard this, all the synagogue were filled with wrath. And they rose up and put him out of the city, and led him to the brow of the hill on which their city was built, that they might throw him down headlong. But passing through the midst of them He went away." (Luke 4:14-30)

When Jesus returned to Nazareth in the power of the Spirit He began to read from Isaiah 61, which predicts the ministry of the Messiah. He announced that He was the fulfillment of this prophecy and that He had come to heal the brokenhearted and set the captives free. Jesus still heals the broken-hearted today. Many people's hearts have been broken by grief rejection and disappointment, but as we give our hurts to Him, He can heal them. He comes to bring good news to those who are sick and hurt. Jesus does not condemn us for our problems. He comes to repair our broken hearts, and release us from the power of sin and from every other oppressive spiritual force that destroys our lives.

The people of Nazareth received Him well and were proud of Him. However when He used the story of Elijah's ministry to Naaman and Elisha's ministry to the woman of Zarephath to show that the Messianic blessings were not just confined to the Jewish people, they turned against Him.

God's mercies are available to all who exercise faith in Him, and His Messiah who is not only the Hope of Israel but also the hope of the world. Though salvation is *from* the Jews, it is *for* all. The religious spirit wants us to believe that God's blessings are just for us, but God's blessings to all who turn to Him. He is the hope not only of Israel but the hope of the entire world. "In Him shall the Gentiles hope." (Isaiah 11:10)

A Prayer

Spirit of the living God that rested upon Jesus, rest on me and equip me to bring good news to the poor everywhere, release to captives everywhere; sight to the blind and liberty to the oppressed.

Chapter Seven

THE JORDAN RIVER

"And the Lord said to Joshua, 'This day I will begin to exalt you in the sight of all Israel, that they may know that, as I was with Moses, so I will be with you. And you shall command the priests who bear the ark of the covenant, When you come to the brink of the waters of the Jordan, you shall stand still in the Jordan.' And Joshua said to the people of Israel, 'Come hither and hear the words of the Lord your God.' And Joshua said, 'Hereby you shall know that the living God is among you and that He will without fail drive out from before you the Canaanites, the Hititites, the Hivites, the Perizites, the Girgashites, the Amorites and the Jebusites...'"

"So when the people set out from the tents, to pass over the Jordan with the priests bearing the ark of the covenant before the people, and when those who bore the ark had come to the Jordan, and the feet of the priests bearing the ark were dipped in the brink of the water.. .the waters coming down from above stood and rose in a heap far off, at Adam.. .and those flowing down towards the sea of the Arabah, the Salt Sea, were whole cut off; and the people passed over opposite

Jericho. And while all Israel were passing over on dry ground, the priests who bore the ark of the covenant of the Lord stood on dry ground in the midst of the Jordan, until all the nation finished passing over the Jordan." (Joshua 3:7-17)

"So Naaman came with his horses and chariots, and halted at the door of Elisha's house and Elisha sent a messenger to him saying, 'Go and wash in the Jordan seven times and your flesh shall be restored, and you shall be clean.' But Naaman was angry and went away saying, 'Behold I thought that he would surely come out to me, and stand and call on the name of the Lord his God, and wave his hand over the place and cure the leper. Are not Abana and Pharpar, the rivers of Damascus, better than all the waters of Israel? Could I not wash in them and be clean?' So he turned and went away in a rage. But his servants came near and said to him, 'My father, if the prophet had commanded you to do some great thing, would you not have done it? How much rather, then, when he says to you, 'Wash, and be clean'?' So he went down and dipped himself seven times in the Jordan, according to the word of the man of God: and his flesh was restored like the flesh of a little; child, and he was clean." (2 Kings 5:9-14)

"John the baptizer appeared in the wilderness, preaching a baptism of repentance for the forgiveness of sins. And there went out to him all the

country of Judea, and all the people of Jerusalem; and they were baptized by him in the river Jordan, confessing their sins. Now John was clothed with camel's hair, and had a leather girdle around his waist, and ate locusts and wild honey. And he preached. saying, 'After me comes He who is mightier than I, the thong of whose sandals I am not worthy to stoop down and untie. I have baptized you with water; but He will baptize you with the Holy Spirit'."

"In those days Jesus came from Nazareth of Galilee and was baptized by John in the Jordan. And when He came up out of the water, immediately He saw the heavens opened, and the Spirit descending upon Him as a dove; and a voice came from heaven, 'Thou art my beloved Son; with thee I am well pleased'."

"The Spirit immediately drove Him out into the wilderness." (Mark 1:4-12)

There are surely more impressive rivers on the earth than the muddy Jordan River as General Naaman of Damascus observed. None however, has witnessed such miraculous events as this divinely chosen river.

Here earth has come into direct contact with the invading acts of heaven. River of the miraculous what sights you have seen from your source in Baneas to your death in the Dead Sea. Your shores are lined with miracles and revelations. You remind us, Jordan River, that our Creator has not left His Creation alone but has involved Himself over and over again with saving actions and direct interventions in the lives and the affairs of men.

The Jordan River was a gateway to the Promised Land for the weary Children of Israel trekking out of Egypt. From the summit of Mount Nebo, Moses gazed over this river to the fertile oasis of the Canaan.

To the Israelis, after the death of Moses, the Jordan River seemed more like an obstacle against entry to their promised land rather than a gateway. However, as they advanced and as the priests went into the water, carrying the Ark of the Covenant of the Lord the waters divided before them. The waters were shut off at the place called Adam and prevented from reaching their dead end in the Dead Sea. This presents us with a fine illustration of what happens when we are given New Life and brought in touch with the glory of God through our High Priest. As we enter into our New Life, the Adam life, which is destined for death, is stopped off and replaced by the eternal life of God.

Not deterred by the obstacles the Israelis at the command of God marched forward, and God moved miraculously to open the way for them. When God calls and we obey, God will move to open up the way before us as we set out to move. Do not be paralyzed from moving if there are obstacles in the way. If God is guiding He will remove all obstacles as we set out to obey. Do not wait until there are no obstacles before you move. If you do, you will never enter your promised land. Begin to move and God will act on your behalf, because the God of Israel is your God too.

It was this river that Elijah crossed before the fiery chariots of God escorted him in to heaven. Here the haughty Syrian general, Naaman finally humbled himself and submitting to Elisha's word became clean as he dipped himself seven times in the river.

But it was in the days of John the baptizer and forerunner that the Jordan saw its most glorious days. As John called the people of Israel to repent and to be baptized and to start anew to serve the Lord, thousands flocked to him from all over the land and all of Jerusalem came to repent and to be baptized. Never in the history of Israel had there been such a massive movement of repentance. John explained that this national act of repentance was to prepare the way for the Messiah.

John saw that the failure of the nation had been due to the presence of sin and the persecution of their neighbors. The people had been looking for a Messiah who would overthrow the yoke of the oppressing nations. The Messiah had to first deal with the sin question. John also saw that it would take more than an act of repentance and a washing away of the sins of the past for the nation to do better. He saw that there would have to be more than a WILL to do better on the part of the people. In addition they needed a new infusion of the Holy Spirit into the people. This is why he announced that the Messiah was not only the Lamb who would bear the sins of the people but also the one who would give them anew spirit. Where John had baptized in water, the Messiah would baptize in the Holy Spirit.

In seeing that the Messianic rule must be preceded by a national repentance and cleansing John was simply echoing a theme of many of the prophets before him. Jeremiah, for example, spoke of the day when God would make a new covenant with His people, write His laws in their hearts and forgive their iniquity (Jeremiah 31:31-35) *"A new heart I will give you, and a new spirit I will put within you; and I will take out the heart of stone and give you heart of flesh. And I will put my spirit within you and cause you to walk in my statutes."* (Ezekiel 36:26-27)

John baptized Jesus at the Jordan and after His baptism he saw the Spirit descend on Him to anoint Him for His ministry of preaching, healing, and for bearing the sins and sicknesses of the world. The Holy Spirit would lead him through humiliation, rejection, and death to resurrection and glory from where He would continue His ministry.

At the Jordan River, this river of separation and cleansing, will you begin a new life? Will you lay aside your old life with its sins and leprosies? Will you turn once more and give your life for the purposes of God? The river Jordan speaks to us today. We can begin anew and live no more for self but for the purposes for which God made us. God in the Messiah has provided forgiveness for all who repent.

Here at the Jordan River we are reminded that there is more than repentance - there is a promised land for us if we follow Yeshua. He will lead us into the Kingdom of God, the kingdom of life and righteousness, peace and joy. He will cut off the river of our own failing Adam life and infuse us with the resurrection life of God. He will equip us for a journey in His footsteps. He will anoint us to minister to others in power and humility and to be fearless of the reproaches of men. He will strengthen us for a journey that may lead through a measure of suffering but will end in glorious union with Him.

At the Jordan River we are invited to lay aside our Adam inheritance, which is laden with the curses and bruises of generations and weakened by sin. Here we can be baptized, burying our old man and letting the life of Jesus come into us to be the only Life that moves us. (Romans 6:6)

Our personal baptism is the funeral service for our Adam life, which was killed with Jesus on the cross. When we accept Him we are baptized into His death. At baptism we let the world know that we are dead to its demands and to the demands of the sin nature that held us captive. Rising from the waters of baptism we are free to respond to God as we come up to live in the power of resurrection life and for His purposes. We are now to be controlled no longer by our Adam nature, which had been chained to sin, but by the resurrected life of Christ, which is chained to righteousness.

The abundant life that Jesus offers is not a religious se]f improvement course. At baptism we lay down Adam and take up Christ to be our only life. We no longer TRY to live a righteous life: or become a righteous person. . . we RECEIVE a righteous life and let His righteousness manifest through us. It is no longer we who live, but Christ who lives in us. Receive a new life; lay down your failing Adam life with its complex past. Be washed of the past. Be a new creation and live as one.

A Prayer

Lord, I repent and turn away from my self-centered life. I ask for a new start. I thank You that my old man has died with You. No longer will I be controlled by my old Adam nature or by the past. I yield myself to be controlled by You. Behold I come to do Your will, O God.

Chapter Eight

MOUNT OF TEMPTATION

"Then Jesus was led by the Spirit into the wilderness to be tempted by the devil. And He fasted forty days and forty nights and afterward he was hungry. And the tempter came and said to Him, 'If you are the Son of God, command these stones to become loaves of bread.' But He answered, 'It is written, man shall not live by bread alone, but by every word that proceeds from the mouth of God. 'Then the devil took him to the holy city and set Him on the pinnacle of the temple, and said to him, 'If you are the Son of God, throw yourself down; for it is written, He will give his angels charge of you and on their hands they will bear you up, lest you strike your foot against a stone.' Jesus said to him, 'Again it is written, you shall not tempt the Lord your God.' Again the devil took him to a very high mountain, and showed him all the kingdoms of the world and the glory of them; and he said to him, 'All these I will give you if you will fall down and worship me.' Then Jesus said to him, 'Be gone Satan.

For it is written, you shall worship the Lord your God, and him only shall you serve.' Then the devil left him, and behold, angels came and ministered to him.'"

"Blessed is the man who endures trial, for when he has stood the test he will receive the crown of life which God has promised to those who love him. Let no one say when he is tempted, 'I am tempted by God,' for God cannot be tempted with evil and he himself tempts no one; but each person is tempted when he is lured and enticed by his own desire. Then desire when it has conceived gives birth to sin; and sin when it is full-grown brings forth death."

The temptations that Jesus, who was "a man like us in all things but sin," endured are the same temptations that every man and woman must face, particularly those who are anointed by the Holy Spirit and wish to serve the Lord. When we think on these temptations we think, not only of spiritual tests that Jesus endured 2000 years ago but of the tests that we face each day.

Four major temptations can be discerned here - four temptations that every spirit-filled son of God will face. The first temptation to "command these stones to become loaves of bread." can be seen as a summary of a temptation that all of us must overcome, the temptation to seek material comfort and satisfaction before obedience to God. Yes, God will supply our every need, but we must first follow Him. No one can follow Him unless he learns to put obedience to God before pleasing himself and seeking material satisfaction.

The second temptation when the devil placed Him at the pinnacle of the temple and asked Him to jump presumptuously, is the temptation to expect the support and sustenance of God without obeying Him. Today, we see many Christians who "do their own thing" and ask God to bless it. God only blesses that which He has ordered. Jesus was facing the temptation to be controlled by His own plans rather than by the plans of God, for the devil knew that if He could sidetrack Jesus from obedience to His Father he would frustrate Jesus' mission. *"I have come down from heaven, not to do my own will but the will of Him who sent me."* (John 6:38)

Many today launch out to do the work of the Lord. They are full of good ideas and plans and schemes for promoting the kingdom of God. Many of these zealous people are moving in presumption, they do not stop to hear what God's plan and directives are. Perhaps they are afraid that if they wait before Him for His instructions they may hear Him say, "I don't need that." How subtle the devil's temptations are to those who are zealous for the Lord. What Jesus faced you and I must face in our own way.

In the third temptation the devil showed Jesus *"all the kingdoms of the world and the glory of them."*

Jesus was being tempted to take over the world for God. How much all of us desire the praises of men and to receive glory and recognition and power in this world. All of this will come in time for Jesus and His church, but it is not these that we pursue but obedience to the Lord.

It is interesting to note that the devil tempts us with things and positions that may be God's will for us. It is not enough for us to know that God wants us to have something or to give us some position or other. The important thing is that we are not seeking these things but are seeking to please Him. He has a timing for everything and first it was necessary for Jesus to suffer many things. Jesus emptied Himself becoming obedient unto death therefore God has high exalted Him. The Father has given Him all the devil tempted Him with . . . but in the right time and the right way. *"Seek first the kingdom of God and His righteousness and all these things will be added on to you,"* says Jesus. The devil says, "God wants you to have glory - go for it!" He would have us bypass the processes in between, and have us pursue the benefits of the kingdom in a selfish way rather than the purposes of God with our lives. Jesus faced all these temptations and resisted them at the very beginning of His mission so that when these temptations recurred in the middle of His ministry He was quickly able to discern and recognize them. How important it is for us to discern the difference between the voice of the devil who speaks through our selfish desires and lusts and the voice of the Holy Spirit. What a master he is at twisting scriptures to deceive us. Those who dedicate themselves to live not for themselves but for God's purposes will have power to overcome as Jesus overcame.

Overarching each of these temptations was the phrase used by the devil in his conversation with Jesus: "IF you are the Son of God..." How often we believers are tempted to do something to prove that God is with us, or that we really are anointed. We can overcome this if we know who and whose we really are. When we know who we are we do not have to prove anything to anyone. We do not act to prove anything we act only to obey and please God.

Note: Many believers having received the new life of the Holy Spirit and having been baptized in the Holy Spirit go through testing experiences where they do not feel as if they are children of God. They wonder if they have been really filled with the Holy Spirit. They begin to have thoughts suggesting bizarre courses of action even suicide. They need not be unduly concerned however, for this is simply the devil talking to them. They do not need to be saved again or to have demons cast out of them. It is simply the devil talking to them as He did to Jesus. Christians should be able to talk back to the devil and say as Jesus did, *"Be gone Satan!"* We need to be able to tell him to stop his deceptive talk and to confess that we are children of God who are choosing to obey and trust God in everything.

A Prayer

Thank You Lord that You have redeemed me and adopted me into Your family. Behold I come to do Your will. I trust that as I do this You will take care of my every need so I am going to spend the rest of my days obeying you. I refuse to use worldly means to achieve apparently godly ends that have not been selected or endorsed by You. I refuse to believe the devil when he lies to me and tries to make me doubt my relationship with God or to lead me to put any other goal or method ahead of Your goal and directives for my life.

Chapter Nine

BETHSAIDA - HOME OF THE FISHERMAN

"And passing along by the Sea of Galilee, he saw Simon and Andrew the brother of Simon casting a net in the sea; for they were fishermen. And Jesus said to them, "Follow me and I will make you become fishers of men." And immediately they left their nets and followed him. And going on a little farther, he saw James the son of Zebedee and John his brother, who were in their boat mending the nets. And immediately he called them; and they left their father Zebedee in the boat with the hired servants, and followed him. (Mark 1: 16-20)

The fishing village of Bethsaida on the North Shore of The Sea of Galilee is the home town of Peter, Andrew, James, John & Philip, the first disciples.

Jesus called ordinary people from the routine of their normal lives to a higher destiny and calling. These men, and those who follow Him would become the instruments of the extension of His mission to the ends of the earth.

61

"Follow Me and I will make you become ...." He does not wait for us to make ourselves something and then follow Him when we are fully prepared. On the contrary He calls us to follow Him and in the following we become what He wants us to be.

"He who believes in me the works that I do He will do also and greater works then these will he do because I go to the Father." (John 14:12) From Bethsaida Jesus began to teach and prepare His disciples to follow in His footsteps, to love as He loved, to act as He acted, do as He did. They in turn would make disciples of all nations *'teaching them to do all that I have taught you to do.'*

All who follow Jesus are not necessarily asked to abandon their normal business but to put the normal business into second place and to become totally available to Him.

What a change took place in the destiny of these first disciples when they encountered Jesus and His calling on their lives! An equally profound change takes place in our destiny when we surrender all to follow Jesus and loose ourselves from the demands and pressures of the world and its agenda to be available to Him.

Today many are content simply to take Jesus as Savior, but few will release their lives to follow Him. The world waits for the mobilizing of tens of thousands of ordinary men and women who will follow Him and to the cause of His Kingdom.

Have you heard Jesus say to you, "Follow Me"? have you decided to follow Jesus? As you stand in this place why not yielded your life to His call to you? He is not looking at your *ability* , but at your *availability*.

Healings At Bethsaida

"And when they had crossed over, they came to land at Gennesaret, and moored to the shore. And when they got out of the boat, immediately the people recognized him, and ran about the whole neighborhood and began to bring sick people on their pallets to any place where they heard he was. And wherever he came, in villages, cities, or country, they laid the sick in the market places, and besought him that they might touch even the fringe of his garment; and as many as touched it were made well.

(Mark 6:53-56)

So powerful was the healing ministry of Jesus that the crowds filled the streets with sick people that they laid in the market place. Bethsaida was one of these cities that were thronged with believers who reached out to Jesus for the healing of sickness. Israel's archaeologists have uncovered today these streets and we can walk on the same stones on which the sick were laid and healed.

"Jesus is the same yesterday today and forever." (Hebrews 4:10) Wherever the word of His healing grace is proclaimed, the healing mercy of Jesus is still received today. Let us never cease to proclaim the might and mercy of the great Physician whose mercies endure forever. Reach out and touch the Lord for your healing.

A Remarkable Healing In Bethsaida

"And he came to Bethsaida; and they brought a blind man to him, and begged him to touch him. And he took the blind man by the hand, and led him out of the town; and when he had spit on his eyes, and put his hands upon him, he asked him if he saw anything. And he looked up, and said, I see men as trees, walking. After that he put his hands again upon his eyes, and made him look up: and he was restored, and saw everyone clearly. And he sent him away to his house, saying, Neither go into the town, nor tell anyone in the town. (Mark 8.22-26)

Jesus healed this blind man with two touches. At first touch he saw - but not clearly. At second touch he saw clearly. This miracle was not only a healing but also a prophetic gesture. When we come to Jesus, He opens our spiritual sight, but as we continue to stay with Him our spiritual sight become more and more clear. We should always ask the Holy Spirit to empower us to see more clearly what Jesus has done and continues to do.

A Prayer

Lord thank You that you love me and are calling me to walk in Your footsteps. I too want to follow You and be an instrument of Your love mercy truth and healing in a world that is full of spiritual blindness. Today I make a quality decision to follow You and to subordinate the interests of career to your call. I choose you as My Manager. I make myself available to you for whatever directions and strategies you have for my life.

'Three things I ask:
To love Thee more dearly,
to see Thee more clearly,
to follow Thee more nearly.'

Chapter Ten

CANA OF GALILEE

"On the third day there was a marriage at Cana in Galilee and the mother of Jesus was there. Jesus also was invited to the marriage with His disciples. When the wine gave out, the mother of Jesus said to Him, 'They have no wine.' And Jesus said to her, 'O woman what have you to do with me? My hour has not yet come.' His mother said to the servants, 'Do whatever He tells you.' Now six stone jars were standing there, for the Jewish rites of purification, each holding twenty or thirty gallons. Jesus said to them, 'Fill the jars with water.' And they filled them up to the brim. He said to them, 'Now draw some out and take it to the steward of the feast.' So they took it. When the steward of the feast tasted the water, now become wine, and did not know where it came from (though the servants who had drawn the water knew), the steward of the feast called the bridegroom and said to him, 'Every man serves the good wine first; and when men have drunk freely, then the poor wine; but you have kept the good wine until now.' This is the

first of His signs Jesus did at Cana in Galilee and manifested His glory; and his disciples believed in Him." (John 2:1-11)

In this quiet village of Cana, Jesus performed His first sign turning water into wine. He has come that our joy may be full. The great quantity of wine that was drawn from the stone jars symbolizes the unlimited joy of the kingdom of God. Jesus is a man of joy. The dwelling place of God is with men, and in this village at this country wedding He manifested the first sign of the happy kingdom He was bringing to men. He loves simple human beings and serves His best wine to them.

This wedding speaks of another wedding, the wedding between Christ and His Bride. The best wine was served last. In these last days we shall receive the greatest blessings of God if we get ourselves ready. The jars were first filled with water then the water became wine. His presence turns the water of ordinary life into wine. Make sure that we invite Him to be a part of our ordinary lives. Some keep God imprisoned behind pearly gates far away, but He wants to be involved in the simple daily matters of our days on earth.

This wedding was on the "third day". A thousand years is as a day with the Lord. We are now in the third millennium since Jesus. The third millennium will be the wedding day. Believers in Jesus should have a special sense of joy because we are getting ready for a wedding of complete union with our Bridegroom who has gone away to prepare a place for us. Some believers have allowed their spiritual wine run out. Offer the master what you have and He will fill your life with new wine. The best wine is reserved for the end days. Do not complain that the wine has run out in the church or in your life. Call on Him for He has kept the best wine until now.

Jesus did not respond immediately to His mother's plea. His hour had not yet come. Yet a few moments later He acts. Jesus is bound to the will of the Father, and He cannot move just on the basis of human need or the plea of His mother. He has to wait until the hour comes for the Father to move, and then He does.

Many believers today spend their time responding to needs, but this does not produce miracles or bring God's blessing. God wants us to be related to Him and not to need. When we are related to Him, then He will relate us to the needs to which He directs us, only then will we see His miracles. Have you come to an end of running around responding to needs? Have you come to a place of rest at the Master's feet, waiting for Him to direct you to the projects and needs He wants you to relate to? Most believers are need oriented and need controlled. Jesus was God oriented and God controlled. This is the secret of miracles. Can you wait for the hour of God?

Jesus waited thirty years for God's moment. How hard it is for us to wait for God's moment. How hard it is for us not to respond to man's need and instead respond to God's plan, which will in the end solve every need.

Mary's last recorded words in the gospels are here: *"Whatever He says to you do it!"* (John 2:5) Her desire was that we follow her Son and His words. What perfect advice. Those who would revere Mary should obey Jesus and His words.

A Prayer

Lord, we acknowledge that we are bound to your timing and will. Cause me to walk in perfect union with your time and plan. Forgive me for being pressured by the urgency of need and the pressure of man. Help me to come into union with your plan and time, and into the flow of your miracles.

Please accept my invitation, Lord Jesus, to be involved in all the daily events of my life. Thank you for your quiet, unseen help that helps me cope with everyday problems and solves so many before I even become aware of them.

Chapter Eleven

CAPERNAUM - CENTER OF JESUS' MINISTRY

"As he entered Capernaum, a centurion came forward to him, beseeching him and saying, "Lord, my servant is lying paralyzed at home, in terrible distress." And he said to him, "I will come and heal him." But the centurion answered him, "Lord, I am not worthy to have you come under my roof; but only say the word, and my servant will be healed. For I am a man under authority, with soldiers under me; and I say to one, 'Go,' and he goes, and to another, 'Come,' and he comes, and to my slave, 'Do this,' and he does it." When Jesus heard him, he marveled, and said to those who followed him, "Truly, I say to you, not even in Israel have I found such faith. I tell you, many will come from east and west and sit at table with Abraham, Isaac, and Jacob in the kingdom of heaven, while the sons of the kingdom will be thrown into the outer darkness; there men will weep and gnash their teeth." And to the centurion Jesus said, "Go; be it done for you as you have believed." And the servant was healed at that very moment.

And when Jesus entered Peter's house, he saw his mother-in-law lying sick with a fever; he touched her hand, and the fever left her, and she rose and served him. That evening they brought to him many who were possessed with demons; and he cast out the spirits with a word, and healed all who were sick. This was to fulfill what was spoken by the prophet Isaiah, "He took our infirmities and bore our diseases." (Matthew 8:5:17)

Capernaum became the center of Jesus ministry and some of his most remarkable teaching and healings, including the healing of the mother of Peter's wife and the Roman centurion who sought healing for his servant. Jesus healed him at a distance with a word of command. He healed by the use of a word of command.

Jesus The Bread Of Life

At Capernaum, Jesus gave some of His most profound teachings.

'So Jesus said to them, "Truly, truly, I say to you, unless you eat the flesh of the Son of man and drink his blood, you have no life in you; he who eats my flesh and drinks my blood has eternal life, and I will raise him up at the last day. For my flesh is food indeed, and my blood is drink indeed. He who eats my flesh and drinks my blood abides in me, and I in him. As the living Father sent me, and I live because of the

Father, so he who eats me will live because of me. This is the bread which came down from heaven, not such as the fathers ate and died; he who eats this bread will live for ever." This he said in the synagogue, as he taught at Capernaum.' (John 6:53-59)

Jesus taught that as we receive physical strength through food we receive spiritual strength by drawing life from Him. Many seek to serve God in their own strength but Jesus is coming to teach, to heal and to forgive but to give us a new heavenly life that will empower us to live as sons and daughters of God.

Do you draw life from Him? If not from what do you draw?

The Judgment Of Capernaum

"Then He began to upbraid the cities where most of His mighty works had been done, because they did not repent. And you Capernaum, will you be exalted to heaven? You shall be brought down to Hades. For if the mighty works done in you had been done in Sodom, it would have remained until this day. But I tell you that it shall be more tolerable on the day of judgment for the land of Sodom than for you."

(Mt. 11:20, 23-24)

Today, exactly as Jesus predicted, all that remains of the lake cities of Galilee that Jesus upbraided, Capernaum, Chorazin and Bethsaida, are ruins. The rocks carry a dim memory of the events that took place in these towns. Capernaum was the center of Jesus ministry. God the Father through Jesus showed that He is at war against all that oppresses mankind - the sickness that binds men's bodies, the demons that bind their minds and spirits, and the ignorance that darkened their minds. The kingdom of God was broke in on these lakeshore people. God was acting to release them from their oppressions. God is not limited by place as He showed the centurion and He is not limited by time. Today He continues to break every yoke as we believe.

Yet there is sadness too recorded in the silent witness of the rocks of Capernaum, for the mighty works did not result in changed hearts and in repentance.

Wherever Jesus went He took authority over the demons and over disease and He has passed on this mandate to His followers of all generations. When blind guides teach that Jesus' miracles of healing are not for today they forfeit any claim to call themselves preachers of the gospel of the kingdom of God. Wherever Jesus' gospel is preached there is healing and deliverance from oppression.

The preaching and bringing of this good news should result in a turning towards God. It is the greatest key to evangelism, for in the presence of the miracles of healing, man is brought face to face with the nature of His God. Where there is healing God is showing Himself to be alive and concerned for the welfare of humanity. If such mighty works as were performed through Jesus at Capernaum did not bring the people to repentance then indeed these people's hearts were hard. We can perhaps understand when people today, who have never heard the gospel of the kingdom of God, or seen the saving actions of God, have not been stirred to repentance, but when people do not repent in the face of such great works they will not be moved by anything.

If the world of today is to be moved to repentance, then the gospel that Jesus preached will have to be preached, not just in word only, but in power. The Scribes spoke words about God and His laws; Jesus brought the power of God to bear on areas of human need. Sickness is not the will of God. We need much prayer that the church will recover its power to bring the healing power of God to bear on the bodies of all those who are oppressed by sickness. May the Holy Spirit open men's hearts and minds to see that their sickness and oppressions have been borne by Jesus.

A Prayer

Remembering the lesson of Capernaum we ask that Your power will be released on earth to bring men to repentance. We ask that we can follow You as closely as Peter and Andrew and James and John. Yes we accept the call to receive your kingdom and to bring your kingdom to others. Father display your power to heal the oppressions of the world. Let the ministry of Jesus be continued through your people today. Stretch forth your hands to heal and to do miracles today.

Chapter Twelve

THE SEA OF GALILEE

"Then He made the disciples get into the boat and go before Him to the other side while He DISMISSED the crowds. And after He dismissed the crowds, He went up into the hills by Himself to pray. When evening came, 1-le was there alone, but the boat by this time was many furlongs distant from the land, beaten by the waves; for the wind was against them. And in the fourth watch of the night He came to them walking on the sea. But when the disciples saw Him walking on the sea, they were terrified saying, 'It is a ghost!' And they cried out for fear. But immediately He spoke to them, saying, 'Take heart, it is I; have no fear'.

"And Peter answered Him, 'Lord, if it is You, bid me come to you on the water.' He said, 'Come.' So Peter got out of the boat and walked on the water and came to Jesus; but when he saw the waves he was afraid and beginning to sink, he cried out, 'Lord, save me.' Jesus immediately reached out his hand and caught him, saying to him, 'O man of little faith, why

did you doubt?' and when they got into the boat the wind ceased. and those in the boat worshipped him, saying, 'truly you are the Son of God.'" (Matthew 14:22-23)

The world was founded on the word of God. Through Jesus, God upholds the universe. God cannot violate his word and His word cannot fail. Peter obeyed Jesus and trusted His word as able to sustain Him in, even in the face of adverse circumstances. Soon however the pressure of circumstances caused him to waver and He began to sink.

We can build our lives on circumstances and live in fear or live a life of trust on God's word and live in serenity even in times of difficulty.

We can trust our whole lives on the word of God and the words of Jesus. All of His followers must learn never to be shaken by circumstances but to build their lives on the sure word of God that can take us through all kinds of storm experiences.

Looking across the pale blue water of the sea of Galilee, hearing the splashing sound of the waves against the shores, remembering the crowds that thronged around this shore to see the Messiah sent by God to ease the pain of mankind and to restore men to the canopy of God's benign protection, the centuries roll away. It is as if the waves washing on the shore have washed away the footprints of 2000 years and have left only the unerasable footsteps of the Master.

Is it 2000 years ago or is it just yesterday that He walked on this shore? For us who believe in Him, He is the same yesterday today and forever, for He is alive and with us today as we remember Him. In our imagination we see and hear the crowds who had come by foot and mule and donkey from as far away as Syria and Lebanon, hungry, unlettered people with the wisdom that comes from simplicity. As great as those crowds were we realize that today as we read these words, His fame has spread even further. Today greater multitudes are touching Him and being touched by Him than ever before. Here in Galilee we are confronted with a figure who appeared and stirred the waters of this sea and healed the bodies of the crowds that gathered there, but we sense that we are in touch not only with a figure from the past but the Lord of the present.

"Then Jesus said, 'Do not be afraid; go and tell my brethren to go to Galilee and there they will see me.

"Now the eleven disciples went to Galilee, to the mountain to which Jesus had directed them. And when they saw Him they worshipped Him; but some doubted. And Jesus came and said to them, 'All authority in heaven and earth has been given to me. Go therefore and make disciples of all nations, baptizing them in the name of the Father and of the Son and of the Holy Spirit, teaching them to observe

all that I have commanded you; and lo, I AM WITH YOU ALWAYS, to the close of the age.'" (Mt. 28:11 16-20)

A PRAYER

Lord, I too want to live a life of faith. I want to obey Your word without fear or doubt. I thank You, Lord, that as I lift my eyes off the storms and problems that surround me, I can behold You and hear Your voice. Then my fear is lifted and my faith restored. I choose this day to walk by faith in Your word.

Chapter Thirteen

THE MOUNT OF THE BEATITUDES

"Seeing the crowds he went upon the mountain, and when he sat down his disciples came to him. And he opened his mouth and taught them saying, 'Blessed are the poor in spirit for theirs is the kingdom of heaven ... Blessed are the peacemakers, for they shall be called sons of God ... Blessed are you when men revile you and persecute you and utter all kinds of evil against you falsely on my account. Rejoice and be glad for your reward is great in heaven, for so men persecuted the prophets that were before you...

Think not that I have come to destroy the law and the prophets; I have not come to abolish them but to fulfill them ... For I tell you unless your righteousness exceeds that of the Scribes and the Pharisees you will never enter the kingdom of heaven. You have heard that it was said to the men of old, 'You shall not kill; and whoever kills shall be liable to judgment." But I say to you that everyone who is angry with his brother shall be liable to judgment.

You have heard that it was said, 'You shall love your neighbor and hate your enemy.' But I say to you, Love your enemies and pray for those who persecute you so that you may be sons of your Father who is in heaven.

Beware of practicing your piety before men in order to be seen by them; for then you will have no reward from your Father who is in heaven.

And in praying do not heap up empty phrases as the Gentiles do; for they think that they will be heard for their many words. . Pray then like this:

Our Father who are in heaven, Hallowed be Thy name. Thy kingdom come, Thy will be done on earth as it is in heaven. Give us this day our daily bread, and forgive us our debts, as we have forgiven our debtors. And lead us not into temptation, but deliver us from evil.

For if you forgive men their trespasses, your heavenly Father also will forgive you; but if you do not forgive men their trespasses, neither will your Father forgive your trespasses.

Do not lay up for yourselves treasures on earth... But lay up for yourselves treasures in heaven where neither moth nor rust consumes and where thieves do not break in and steal. For where your treasure is, there will your heart be also. Therefore, I tell you, do not be anxious about your life, what you shall eat or what you shall drink, nor about your body

*what you shall put on.. .Consider the lilies of the field,
how they grow; they neither toil nor spin yet I tell you,
even Solomon in all his glory was not arrayed like one
of these. For the Gentiles seek all these things, and
your heavenly Faber knows that you need them all. But
seek first his kingdom and his righteousness, and all
things shall be yours as well.*

*Judge not that you be not judged. For with the
measure you pronounce you will be judged.*

*Ask and it will be given to you; seek and you
will find; knock and it will be opened to you.*

*Beware of false prophets, who come in sheep's
clothing but inwardly are ravenous wolves.., you will
know them by their fruits.*

*Everyone then who hears these words of mine
and does them will be like a wise man who built his
house upon the rock."*(Matt. Ch. 5 & 6)

On the hills of Galilee before simple crowds
who had come great distances on foot to hear His
words and be healed of their diseases these sublime
words were spoken. Jesus is that prophet of which
Moses spoke, who would come after him whose words
must be heeded. Here is a new Mount Sinai, a new
giving of the law. It is not so much a new law that
Jesus is giving but the law interpreted in terms of
attitudes rather than in terms of ordinances. Before this
law of Christ all stand convicted. None can say he has
perfectly fulfilled all these words of Jesus.. .all of us

stand in need of the forgiveness He offers. Having received and given to others the forgiveness He offers, and having received the impartation of His spirit we are equipped to live this way of life set out for us in this discourse.

Here is the way for all men to live on earth in union with God. This is the way all disciples of Jesus must live: total forgiveness towards all; goodness toward our enemies.. .complete and carefree trust in God as our loving Father, prayer to Him, not only for our own needs but for His kingdom and blessing to fall on all. Here there is no religiosity just simple direct and sincere prayer to God. Here self-assertion is replaced with simple carefree trust, evil is overcome not by force but by forgiveness.

The kingdom being portrayed here is not just some fanciful ideal, or something that is to be practiced by us in some future age, but is the way of living we are called to today. *"He who hears these words of mine and does them"* is the man who is building his life the right way.

It is clear that Jesus asks us to live by the teachings of this sermon. Yet, He also knows that it is *impossible* for us to live by them. It is only possible for us to live this way if we acknowledge our inability and failure to live this way. Then by faith we can draw life from God who gives life to the "lilies of the field and the birds of the air" to empower us to live this way.

Jesus not only gives the teaching but He empowers us to live by it as we lean on Him by faith and receive the empowerment of the Holy Spirit.

How upside down the words of Jesus are to the philosophies of today, and the principles for successful living that are taught today in the world. How restless is the way of those who push their way in life. How beautiful the way of those who trust and obey their Father. The way of Jesus is not for the "wishy-washy" or the passive. We are to "ask, seek, knock" to find this kingdom. It is not for the passive or the timid. Because of the evil that is in the world those who live this way will have to endure persecution and misunderstanding. They will have to resist evil and overcome it by the greater strength of goodness and forgiveness. They will have to hold on to their trust and to their principles when pressures from every side would cause them to live the lower way. Those who do not seek to live this way are simply those who call Him Lord without making Him Lord. Such ones cannot represent Him to the world.

Few have lived these sayings of Jesus. Those who do shine like lights. They have found the kingdom of God.

Forgive, Forgive, Forgive

The heart of the teaching of Jesus consisted in the message of forgiveness. We are to receive forgiveness from God, and give forgiveness to others, not just occasionally but constantly.

Each of us has his rights, but the mandate to forgive is greater than the right to have our own way. Forgiveness is extended not only to those who apologize but also to enemies, and to those who oppose us.

Lack hinders the Lord's forgiveness and blessing flowing to us, blocks our prayers, steals our joy, and wounds our bodies.

On the cross Jesus forgave all who were responsible for His execution. On the day of His resurrection He dispensed forgiveness to His disciples and commanded them to forgive sins. In the Sermon on the Mount He insisted that forgiveness of all was the condition of enjoying the Father's forgiveness and blessing.

The greatest lesson He imparted to us was the message of God's forgiveness of our sins and our obligation to forgive all who have mistreated us in any way. Those who do not forgive, no matter how much religion they practise, how zealous they are for the cause of God, cannot represent the truth of God.

Followers of Jesus are not simply called to forgive frequently but to forgive continually. It has to be priority number one. As we give forgiveness we receive it, and as we receive it we are empowered to give it. It is sad when Jesus' followers fight among each other, speak evilly against those who do not agree with them, or allow ethnic, religious and political differences to block the flow of forgiveness and love.

There is a river of love in the heart of God; it flows into our hearts as we receive His forgiveness and it flows out into the world as we give wholesale forgiveness to everyone, even those who have injured us, treated us unjustly, differ from us politically or religiously. God's kingdom will come on earth as this kind of forgiveness becomes our way of life.

A Prayer

Father we trust you. Forgive us where we have not lived these principles. From now on with your help we will live this way. We choose this way. Lord, I accept your total forgive-ness. I extend that forgiveness to everyone who has injured or disappointed me; to every family member and to anyone who differs from me in political or religious opinions.

Chapter Fourteen

CAESAREA PHILIPPI/BANEAS

"Now when Jesus came into the district of Caesarea Philippi, He asked His disciples, 'Who do men say that the Son of man is?' And they said, 'Some say, John the Baptist, others say Elijah, and others Jeremiah or one of the prophets.' He said to them, 'But who do you say that I am?' Simon Peter replied, 'You are the Christ, the Son of the living God.' And Jesus answered him, 'Blessed are you Simon Bar Jona! For flesh and blood has not revealed this to you, but my Father who is in heaven.'" (Mt. 16:13-17)

"And I tell you, you are Peter, and on this rock I will build my church and the powers of hell shall not prevail against it." (Mt. 16:13-18)

The Jordan River has its source at Baneas, in the Caesarea Philippi area. The melting snows from Mount Hermon flow down to Baneas. Here we see the water flow from the rocks and begin to form the Jordan, which is the source of most of the fresh water supply for the land of Israel.

In the same rocks at Baneas one can see, carved out of the mountain, grottos which once held statues erected to the "god" Pan, from which the name: Baneas is derived. It was here at this location that Jesus chose to openly make His definitive claim to be more than a prophet, the Messiah, and The Rock from which the stream of blessing would flow out to Israel bless the world.

Whenever we confess Jesus as Savior and Messiah we begin to build our lives on Him the Rock. When Jesus said *"on this Rock I will build my church,"* He was referring to Himself. *"Ascribe greatness to our God! The Rock, his work is perfect; for all his ways are justice. A God of faithfulness and without iniquity, just and right is he."* (Deut 32: 3-4) David says that "the Rock of Israel" spoke to him. (2 Sa 23:3) Jesus uses this as a messianic title referring to Himself. He claimed to be the Rock of Israel and of those who would believe in Him – His church.

In Greek the same word is used for rock and stone, but in Hebrew two words are used one "tsur" which means "massive rock" and the other "eben" which means "stone". Peter became a stone whose life is built on the rock Jesus. The church of Jesus is built on Jesus the Rock of Israel not Peter. Peter himself writes: *" and like living stones be yourselves built into a spiritual house, to be a holy priesthood, to offer spiritual sacrifices acceptable to God through Jesus Christ.* (1Pe 2:5) He became a stone whose life was built on the rock, Jesus.

At Baneas Jesus challenged the pagan religion of the nations symbolized by the statue of Pan, when He said that the gates of hell would not prevail against His church? Here, He was claiming to be the Messiah of Israel against whom the powers of darkness and unenlightened empires would not prevail. As death issued forth from the worship of Pan, life and living water would come from Him. There is only one true God but there are many demons. The pagans worshipped demons thinking them to be gods. Jesus comes to restore us to the worship of the One true God, who is the Creator, the God of Abraham Isaac and Jacob ad the 'God and Father of Our Lord Jesus Christ". Worship of any other spiritual force is idolatry and destructive. It must be resisted and renounced if we are to follow Jesus and inherit the fullness of life.

Today, as in the years of His earthly ministry, men debate among themselves who Jesus is or was. Is He another prophet, another carpenter, just another citizen of Nazareth, another rabbi with illusions of grandeur? Men have always had many opinions as to who Jesus was. Peter was inspired to say that Jesus was the Messiah and the Son of God. Jesus explained that it took a revelation from heaven to see this. Only the eyes of faith, the eyes of the spirit can see who Jesus really is. One cannot learn who he is from a doctrine, catechism or Sunday school class. One cannot be forced into belief in Jesus or argued into belief in Him. Though we do well to show people the evidence, in the end it is God Himself who removes the veil. Behind the appearances He is more, He is the Messiah from whom blessings are to flow to all men.

Who Are You?

No doubt there are many different ways in which people describe you. You have many roles that you fill. There are many ways by which people could describe you. You could be described as the person who lives on such and such a street, is a member of a particular family, and works at a particular job. Others may describe you as one of 6 billion people living on earth!! All these may be accurate descriptions of who you are in the natural, but if that is all you know about who you are, you are going to have a severe identity crisis. If you have been adopted into God's family, you have received a share of the nature of God and you are a Son of God alive on the earth with an assignment from your Heavenly Father.

Once we know who we are when we are in Christ, we do not concern ourselves as much with what people say we are, or how they describe us. We do not take our self-image from what they say about us, or from our sociological position. We take our self-image from what the Holy Spirit and the Word of God shows us that we are. Many believers fail to put on this new self-image and so they continue to respond to the image others project on them. They never learn to function as the Sons of God they are, and to get on with "the Father's business" for their lives.

Jesus did not respond or live from others' opinions of who He was. He knew that He was the Messiah and that He was the unique Son of God. He knew He had a mission to accomplish and His whole life was centered around this.

We can see ourselves not according to our cultural identity but according to our heavenly identity. Then no matter what we are in the eyes of people we will know that we are God's children with a work to do on earth. When people do not know in their hearts their real value, they are constantly trying to prove that they are important by what they own, or by what they do, or by who they know. Knowing who we are in Christ frees us from all of this so that we can live in response to God's call on our lives.

A Prayer

Yes Lord, I believe that thou art the Christ the Son of the living God, and that because of you Iam sharing in your nature so that I too am a Son of God. This day I put on the wind of Christ and I dedicate myself to live in the world not to impress the world but to carry out the work you have given me to do.

Chapter Fifteen

THE MOUNTAIN OF TRANSFIGURATION

"And after six days, Jesus took with Him Peter and James and John, and led them up a high mountain apart by themselves, and He was transfigured before them, and His garments became glistening, intensely white, as no fuller on earth could bleach them. And there appeared to them Elijah with Moses, and they were talking to Jesus. And Peter said to Jesus, 'Master, it is well that we are here; let us make three booths, one for you and one for Moses and one for Elijah.' For he did not know what to say, for they were exceedingly afraid. And a cloud overshadowed them, and a voice came out of the cloud, 'This is my beloved Son; listen to Him.' And suddenly looking around they no longer saw anyone with them but Jesus only." (Mark 9:2-8)

As Moses and Elijah appeared transfigured with Jesus, Peter wanted to construct a booth for each of these anointed messengers, but the voice of the Father was heard saying, "This is my beloved Son; listen to Him." The glory of the Law and the prophets (represented by Moses and Elijah) was being eclipsed

95

and surpassed by the brighter light of God's beloved Son. The disciples of Jesus were being called by the Father to move from the realm of being guided by law to the realm of the kingdom of God which they could enter if they followed Jesus and be guided by His Spirit.

Moses had led the people of Israel to the threshold of the promised land of Canaan, so the Law of Moses had led the people of Israel to the threshold of the Kingdom of God and the new Joshua (Yeshua) was leading them into the reality, promises, blessings and life of the Kingdom of God. Joshua fulfilled Moses work by leading the Israelites into the land of Promise. Similarly Jesus fulfills Moses work by leading us into the Kingdom of God

As Jesus said, *"The law and the prophets were UNTIL John; since then the good news of the kingdom of God is preached and everyone enters it violently."* (Luke 16:16)

"Now before faith came we were confined under the law, kept under restraint until faith should be revealed. So that the law was our custodian UNTIL Christ came, that we might be justified by faith. But now that faith has come, we are no longer under a custodian; for in Christ Jesus you are all sons of God through faith" (Galatians 3:23-26)

"Moses had foretold that the Lord would raise up for them a prophet like you (Moses) from among

their brethren, and I will put my words in his mouth, and he shall speak to the all that I command him. And whoever will not give heed to my words which he shall speak in my name, I myself will require it of him." (Numbers 18:18-19)

Now at the Mountain of Transfiguration, Jesus is showing His most intimate disciples that He is not simply a great prophet on an equal footing with Moses and Elijah, but that He completes them and surpasses them. They brought the nation to the threshold of the Kingdom of God and He will take all who follow Him closely into that Kingdom. We are to move from obedience to the Law of Moses to obedience to the law of the Spirit of life, the Law of Christ.

Many God-fearing people today are like Peter who wanted to build a tabernacle for Moses and Elijah along with Jesus. They want to have Jesus AND Moses. They want to obey Jesus and follow Him, while at the same time clinging on to the security of tutors and guardians, external rules and traditions. This creates double mindedness in them and prevents further progress into the kingdom of God. They are like someone doing the splits.

The transition from Moses to Jesus can be compared to the transition a young woman makes when she leaves the security and protection of her father's house to marry her husband and follow him down the road of life. If the husband is God's true choice for her he can be trusted and their new life will be blessed. It is not that the father removes his daughter from his protection, or that she is left without protection, but that the Father hands her over to a new and different sort of protection, the protection of her husband. So now God is calling the Jewish people from the righteous *restraint* of the law of Moses to the righteous *life* of the kingdom of the Messiah.

Jesus did not criticize Moses or Elijah; in fact they were seen to be with Him in glory. He simply led His disciples to the fulfillment of what they saw. We thank God for those who have had the role of tutor and guardians in our lives. Our new obedience now is not primarily to them but to the Messiah Jesus who fulfills their teachings and takes us the rest of the way to the Father.

For Jew and Gentile access to the fullness of God's blessings is now through the grace of God purchased by Messiah Jesus. By faith Abraham was blessed and by faith his offspring shall receive blessing.

Moses had prophesied: *"That Lord your God will raise up for you a prophet like me from among you, for your own brothers. You must listen to him ... I will put my words in his mouth, and he will tell them everything I command him. If anyone does not listen to my words that the prophet speaks in my name, I myself will call him to account."* (Deut. 18:15,18-19)

Here on the Mount of Transfiguration (which most believe to be Mount Hermon) the voice of God is heard saying that Jesus is the prophet to whom they must listen; and with this the Law and the prophets agree. *"This is my Beloved Son ... listen to Him."*

The transition from Moses to Jesus has not been an easy one for most Jewish people to make, partly due to Christian misrepresentation of the meaning of this transition. It does not mean that the promises of blessing to the Jewish people have been revoked, nor does it mean their call has been withdrawn, nor that they have to forsake their Jewishness. As the apostle Paul, that most misunderstood of Jews, writes, *"'God has not rejected His people whom He foreknew ... the gifts and call of God are irrevocable."* (Rom. 11:2, 29)

The transition from Moses to Jesus does not mean that the just standards of the law have been abandoned, indeed Jesus calls us to an even higher standard of righteousness than Moses. It simply means that through the gift of the Spirit the law of external rules and ordinances is being fulfilled by the writing of the law of the Spirit of Life in men's hearts. This transition is for those who realize that through their conduct they were unable to establish their own righteousness under the law. We must recognize our need to receive the gift of forgiveness from all transgressions along with a new heart of righteousness.

"Behold the days are coming, says the Lord, when I will make a new covenant with the house of Israel and the house of Judah, not like the covenant which I made with their fathers when I took them by the hand to lead them out of the land of Egypt, my covenant which they broke, though I was their husband, says the Lord. But this is the covenant which I will make with the house of Israel after those days, says the Lord: I will put my laws within them, and I will write it upon their hearts; and I will be their God, and they shall be my people. And no longer shall each man teach his neighbor and teach his brother, saying, 'Know the Lord' for they shall all know me, from the least of them to the greatest, says the Lord; for I will forgive their iniquity, and I will remember their sin no more." (Jeremiah 31:31-34)

A Prayer

Father, thank you for giving us your Son to be our Shepherd and Guide, our leader and pattern. Jesus, we forsake all to follow you, thanking you for the companions you give us to help us on the way. We decide to follow You, to obey Your teachings and Your call.

Chapter Sixteen

JERICHO

"Then Joshua rose early in the morning and the priests took up the ark of the Lord. And the seven priests bearing seven trumpets of ram's horns before the ark of the Lord passed on blowing the trumpets continually; and the armed men went before them, and the rear guard after the ark of the Lord while the trumpets blew continually. And the second day they marched around the city once, and returned into the camp. So they did for six days.

On the seventh day they rose early at the dawn of the day, and marched around the city in the same manner seven times: it was only on that day that they marched around the city seven times. And at the seventh time, when the priests had blown the trumpets Joshua said to the people, 'Shout: for the Lord has given you the city.' ... So the people shouted, and the trumpets were blown. As soon as the people heard the sound of the trumpet, the people raised a great shout, and the wall fell down flat ... and they took the city."
(Joshua 6:16, 20)

Before Joshua led his people into the land of promise, he had an encounter with the Commander of the Lord's army. (Joshua 5:15) This commander is the Lord of Hosts, the Lord Jesus himself. Joshua asked Him which side He was on and He answered in a most unusual way: "No!" God was not on the side of the Israelis or the Canaanites. He does not take sides. He has His own plan. It was Joshua's responsibility to align Himself with God's plan. God had a plan to bring the children of Israel into the Land He promised them. Joshua was simply cooperating with this plan and so was assured of victory.

Today God has brought the people of Israel back to the Land of Promise once again as He promised. Many nations oppose this. They really are not opposing Israel they are opposing the plan of God. They do not believe that God has a plan in history, or that He is using the Jewish people to accomplish His plan. They are blind to this and so oppose Israel and His plan. The responsibility of all of us is to not to co-opt God to our side but to line our whole life up with Him and with His purposes. As we do this we will see His miracles released. Are you on His side? As we come to Jericho let's make sure we are on His side

Our entry into the kingdom of God has many parallels to the Israelite's entry into the promised land. We become citizens of the kingdom of God when we receive the forgiveness of sins and the New Life of the

Holy Spirit, but we still have to press our way into the kingdom of God. There are barriers that must be surmounted, old thoughts that must be cast down, selfishness to be overcome, and tests to be met. We move on into this kingdom with determination, as the presence of God goes before us. Though we move on by our own will and obedience, we look to God to give the victory in every situation.

Many Christians lack that determination to enter the kingdom of God, to put on the ways of Christ and to put off the old ways.

They will be like those who "perished in the wilderness."

Today, throughout: the nations, God is raising up a generation who are determined to "possess the land," to enter into the fullness of their inheritance. They do not count the cost or the inconvenience involved. They will not allow selfishness or wrong ideas or the forces of evil, or religious traditions, hold them back from their birthright. A generation is being raised up that will go further on in the kingdom of God than any previous generation of believers. This is the generation to go in all the way. God is looking for those who will be overcomers.

The book of Revelation speaks of seven trumpets after which Babylon will fall and *"the kingdom of this world will become the kingdom of our Lord and of His Christ.* (Rev. 11:15) Right now we are like Joshua's army surrounding the earth. Soon all that is not of God will collapse and the earth will become the inheritance of the meek who will reign uprightly with their King on the earth.

"As we wait for the 'seventh day,' let us catch the vision!"

Jesus Comes to Jericho

Jesus came to Jericho on His journey to Jerusalem. On one occasion

"He entered Jericho and was passing through. And there was a man named Zaccheus; he was the chief tax collector and rich. AND HE SOUGHT TO SEE WHO JESUS WAS, but could not on account of the crowd, because he was small of stature. So he ran on ahead and climbed up into a sycamore tree to see him for he was to pass that way. And when Jesus came to the place, he looked up and said to him, 'Zaccheus, make haste and come down; for I must stay at your house today.' So he made haste and came down, and received him joyfully. And when they saw it they all murmured, 'He has gone in to be the guest of a man who is a sinner.' ... And Jesus said to him, 'Today salvation has come to this house, since he also is a son of Abraham. For the son of man came to seek and to save the lost'" (Luke 19:1-7,9)

This man really wanted to see Jesus, but he could not because of the crowd and because of his small stature. So he climbed a tree. So great was his desire to see Jesus, that he forgot all about his dignity and the fact that he was a prominent, wealthy man. Because he was able to leave those things to the side, he saw Jesus and Jesus came to his house.

The true picture of Jesus has often been obscured by those who stand around Him. Many use this as an excuse to reject His claims. We need to look over the heads of the crowds and see Jesus as He really is. If we do that He will come bringing salvation to our house. Many have a relationship with Jesus through the crowd that surrounds Him, but He wants us to see and know Him personally and directly. He never rejects anyone who seeks Him on the basis of their social status or lack of it or on the basis of how wicked their life has been before they met Him.

Still other are so sufficient in themselves the t they do not realize they need the Savior to come to their house.

"And as they went out of Jericho, a great crowd followed him. And behold, two blind men sitting by the roadside, when they heard that Jesus was passing by, cried out, "Have mercy on us, Son of David!" The crowd rebuked them, telling them to be silent; but they cried out the more, "Lord, have mercy on us, Son of David!" And Jesus stopped and called them, saying, "What do you want me to do for you?" They said to him, "Lord, let our eyes be opened." And Jesus in pity

touched their eyes, and immediately they received their sight and followed him. (Matthew 20:29-34)

These two blind received their sight because they were determined to receive the benefits that Jesus could bring. Many assume that God's blessing automatically come to us. But we must cry out for them. He responds to those who cry out to Him and who engage their wills in seeking Him. We must continue to cry out for all His benefits to come to us and for Him to give us spiritual sight. Open our eyes Lord that we may see. Jesus asked the blind men: *"What do you want me to do for you?"* He asks you the same. Are you asking Him for anything or has your spiritual life become a vague wishing for the best?

A Prayer

Dear Jesus, I want to see you and to know you for myself, but sometimes I am made to feel that I am not important enough or good enough for you to come near me. I want to put out of my life all that is a hindrance to you. I lay aside my dignity. Please come to my house and stay with me always. Let me always have time for those that the world regards as insignificant or not good enough for you to concern yourself with. Help me to go with you as you seek and save those who are lost in the crowd.

Lord we want to enter into the fullness of our birthright. We know that as we move on it will not all be easy or automatic. We stand against walls of selfishness that have blocked our further entry into your kingdom and we command them to fall. We stand against walls of tradition that have veiled your purpose from us. We stand against every demonic force and physical force that would hinder our walking on into greater union with you, and we command all these walls to fall.

Chapter Seventeen

THE POOL OF BETHESDA HOUSE OF MERCY

"Now there is in Jerusalem by the Sheep Gate a pool, in Hebrew called Bethzatha, which has five porticoes. In these lay a multitude of invalids, blind, lame, paralyzed waiting for the moving of the water; for an angel of the Lord went down at certain seasons into the pool and troubled the water; whoever stepped in first after the troubling of the water was healed of whatever disease he had. One man was there who had been ill for thirty-eight years. When Jesus saw him and knew that he had been there a long time, he said to him, 'Do you want to be healed?' The sick man answered him, 'Sir, I have no man to put me into the pool when the water is troubled, and while Jam going another steps down before me.' Jesus said to him, 'Rise, take up your pallet, and walk,' And at once the man was healed, and he took up his pallet and walked" (John 5:2-9)

Such commotion at the pool of Bethesda! It is the day when the angel will trouble the water and one person can get healed. But here is an enfeebled man

109

lying on a pallet too weak to elbow his way through the crowd to be the one first into the water and to be healed. Surely he knew that he was not going to be the one to be healed in the water. He lies there without much faith or hope. Perhaps he is content to be a spectator to a healing and never to be healed himself. He has been sick for thirty-eight years; he is hardly going to be healed now. Just to know that God heals now and again is a certain comfort.

The pool of Bethesda is by the Sheep Gate, for it was here the sheep were washed before they were brought to the temple to be sacrificed. Among the smells of animals into the milling throng crowded near the pool, comes Jesus. *"Do you want to be healed."?* What a strange question, yet how appropriate. Today thousands flock to healing meetings rejoicing to see other healed, but perhaps they do not want to be healed themselves. After thirty-eight years being sick can become a way of life. Today there are many who do not want to be sick., but do not want to be well either for they have disability pensions they will lose if they get healed. Jesus is looking for those who really want His intervention. It costs to be sick, but it costs to be well also. This man, however, really wants to be healed. Jesus said to *him "Rise, take up your bed and walk."* To move into the Lord's salvation we must rise and walk away from our old way of life into the new life with its new responsibilities.

With Jesus there, he can stand up, walk and leave his old sick life behind. When Jesus comes, healing is no longer a rare event for the especially fortunate ones. With Him there is no being lost in the crowd. He sees us., and moves in compassion to restore us to healthy living. As the man begins to stand up, he finds to his overwhelming joy that he can walk. As he begins to take up his bed and walk he finds the strength to do so. Faith is not a matter of passive waiting but of moving at the Lord's command. Jesus has made healing no longer a rare event but an every day miracle for those who will walk out at Hisword.

Jesus sees us in whatever anguish, suffering, or sickness we may be in. He doesn't condemn us for being sick or weak but reaches in not only to sympathize with us but to heal us.

But why did Jesus not heal everyone at the pool of Bethesda as He had done at Capernaum? He could only do what HisFather directed Him to do. When the Spirit of God directs Him to heal one man, He heals one man; and when the Spirit releases Him to heal the whole crowd He heals the whole crowd. He is not a worker of lawlessness He only moves and acts as directed. What restraint and obedience we see in Jesus. But why did God permit Him to heal only one man at Bethesda? That is beyond our knowledge and yours. What we do know is that there is perfect provision for healing and wholeness in the will of God. Between the exercise of faith and the experience of the results in our bodies there may be a time lapse.

We have all heard it said that "God helps those who help themselves." But the man at the pool was helpless. There was no one to put him in the water. Today many cannot reach a hospital or afford the treatment of a doctor. God has sent Jesus to help the helpless. Rise and be healed.

A Prayer

Lord, I cry out to you for your touch in my life. I want to be whole in spirit, soul and body. Thank you for coming not only to bear my sins but also my sicknesses. I want to be whole, to leave my sickness behind me and to lead a fruitful life for you. Thank you that you have made healing to be "the children's bread."

Chapter Eighteen

BETHANY - THE HOME OF THE POOR

"And while he was at Bethany in the house of Simon the leper, as he sat at table, a woman came with an alabaster flask of ointment of pure nard, very costly, and broke the flask and poured it over his head. But there were some who said to themselves indignantly, 'Why was the ointment thus wasted? For this ointment might have been sold for three hundred denarii, and given to the poor.' And they reproached her. But Jesus said, 'Let her alone: why do you trouble her? She has done a beautiful thing to me. For you always have the poor with you, and whenever you will you can do good to them; but you will not always have me. She has done what she could; she has anointed my body beforehand for burying. And truly I say to you, wherever the gospel is preached in the whole world, what she has done will be told in memory of her.'"

"Then Judas Iscariot, who was one of the twelve, went to the chief priests in order to betray him

to them. And when they heard it they were glad, and promised to give him money." (Mark 14:3-11)

"Now as they went on their way, he entered a village; and a woman named Martha received him into her house. And she had a sister called Mary who sat at the Lord's feet and listened to His teaching. But Martha was distracting with much serving: and she went to him and said, 'Lord do you not care that my sister has left me to serve alone? Tell her then to help me.' But the Lord answered her, 'Martha, Martha you are anxious and troubled about many things; one thing is needful. Mary has chosen the good portion, which shall not be taken away from her.'" (Luke 10:38-41)

The whole purpose of creation consists in this: that God, whose nature is love has sought to share His love with a people in His own image, who in turn would respond to His love. Of course we are to remember the poor and faithfully carry out our daily tasks but our greatest responsibility is to love God, to spend time with Him and to listen to His teaching. As we relate to Him, He may direct us to specific needs. Time and money spent to seek, find and worship the Lord directly is the greatest service we can do for Him. Many will say: "But I serve and love God by loving and serving my fellow mart." That is good and necessary, but it is not a substitute for the direct loving and worship of Him. This is His greatest need in the earth today.

The people of this age measure everything in terms of production and money. These are necessary components of life, even for the most spiritual. The Christian's life, however, can never be centered around work, money, and needs. Many believers today are on a treadmill that reduces life to work and money; even Christian workers can be "distracted with much serving." Mary of Bethany and the woman of Bethany with the flask of nard (possibly one and the same. person) teach us a different message about money, value, worth and measurement. Our lives are to center around God Himself rather than godly work. We have been created for His good pleasure and all the other components of life, work, family, helping the poor, improving society, are all to flow Out of this center. The spokes of the wheel are no substitute for the hub.

Mary had it right. The woman with the flask of nard had it right. Have you and I got it right? Jesus wants our service, but He regards our personal love for Him as more valuable. The lady poured the costly nard on Jesus' head. Perhaps it represented her life savings. The fragrance covers Jesus, fills the room, and as the lady returns to her ordinary duties the fragrance that is on Jesus is on her. There is a fragrance on the life of the one who sits with Jesus which carries over into the whole of their lives. It costs to worship. It costs to have your life to become truly centered around your love for the Lord rather than around career work, service, and money. Man measures by production, God measures by love.

Love is expensive. To the minds of those who are production. money and project oriented much of the actions which love inspires may seem extravagant and wasteful. We may think it a waste that someone would spend time and money in coming apart to be with the Lord and with His people. Those with the measuring rods of the world think it a waste that a person's talents and years are spent taking care of a sick relative or in a situation of obscurity with little visible productivity. In those years of apparent waste, the principle of the alabaster jar of fragrance may be in operation. That apparent waste releases the fragrance of the Lord's life in the believer. Has your life been broken and poured out before Him?

The woman with the jar of nard is the first disciple to accept the necessity of Jesus' death. Jesus explained that she had anointed Him for burial. She anoints Him for burial and she herself is thereby anointed with the same fragrance. When we see the necessity of Jesus' death we see the necessity of the death of our own outer independent self-life. As the alabaster jar has to be broken for the fragrance of the nard to be released; so we who have received the life of the Spirit within us, must be willing for the plans, the goals, and even the strengths of the outer man to be

Chapter Nineteen

LAZARUS' TOMB

"Now when Jesus came, he found that Lazarus had already been in the tomb four days. . .. Martha said to Jesus, 'Lord if you had been here my brother would not have died. And even now I know that whatever you ask from God, God will give you.' Jesus said to her 'Your brother will rise again.' Martha said to him, 'I know that he will rise again, in the resurrection at the last day.' Jesus said to her, 'I am the resurrection and the life; he who believes in me, though he die, yet shall he live, and whoever lives and believes in me shall never die. Do you believe this?' She said to him, 'Yes, Lord; I believe that you are the Messiah, Son of God, he who is coming into the world.'"

"Then Jesus, deeply moved, again, came to the tomb: it was a cave, and a stone lay upon it. Jesus said, 'Take away the stone. Martha, the sister of he dead man, said to him, 'Lord, by this time there will be

an odor, for he has been dead four days.' Jesus said to her, 'Did I not tell you that if you would believe you would see the glory of God?' So they took away the stone. And Jesus lifted up His eyes and said, 'Father, I thank thee that thou hast heard me. I knew that thou hearest me always, but I have said this on account of the people standing by, that they may believe that thou didst send me.' When he said this, he cried with a loud voice, 'Lazarus, come out. The dead man came out, his hands and feet bound with bandages, and his face wrapped with a cloth. Jesus said to them, 'Unbind him and let him go.''' (John 11:17-27; 38-44)

"But God, who is rich in mercy, out of the great love with which he loved us, even when we were dead through our trespasses, made us alive together with Christ..." (Ephesians 2:4)

Jesus has come to put resurrection life in us *today*. He IS the resurrection and the life. He came to put this wonderful resurrection life into us who were dead in our sins. This life is righteous, joyful, peaceful and full of health. Jesus came from heaven to put resurrection life into a dying and dead world. He has come not to condemn the sin and the death, but the fill the dead with life.

Jesus spoke life into the dead Lazarus and commanded him to come forth to a new life. *"Did I not tell you that if you would believe, you would see the glory of God?"* The glory of God is to put His resurrection life into man.

Today the world is filled with more and more people who have tasted of that resurrection life but there are still billions of people who while they live physically are dead. Their spirits that were made to know God, love him, and walk with Him, are dead. We were all born into this condition but Jesus has come to make us come alive and live before God. He came not to start a new religion but to put His Resurrection Life into all men.

Jesus' heart yearns for those who are dead spiritually. He loved us even when we were dead; and in this condition He found us and helped us. He does not give up on ANYONE, or withhold His love from them. Why should we?

After Jesus had spoken life into Lazarus, though he came to life, he was still bound in his grave cloths, with a veil over his face.

This is the condition of many believers today. They have received eternal life from Jesus, but they remain bound by the trappings of their dead life. These trappings may be old habit patterns, old thoughts and fears or human traditions. In such persons the life of the Spirit wants to move in one direction but is hindered from doing so because of the binding trappings of the old life. So Jesus has to speak another word: *"Unbind him, and let him go."* He calls us to come free from the limits and habit patterns of our old manner of life to walk fully into the new life He opens before us.

It is not enough simply to receive the new resurrection life within us. Jesus wants to give us a whole new way of living, and to open up an entirely new set of possibilities for us. How unfortunate when many who have been filled with resurrection life are unable to walk away from their past way of living into the fullness of their new life. Jesus' command however, gives us power not only to come alive, but to walk free from all the evil controls and influences of our old life.

Christians, those who have received the resurrection life of Jesus into themselves., do not have to be bound and held by the sins, the traumas and the limitations of the past. We can simply leave those things behind and walk away from them. Today many struggle and wrestle with the problems that held them bound in their old life. They spend their time exploring and comparing one another's bandages, and in the process they get entangled with their old problems. Jesus calls us to drop our bandages and to walk away from the binding habits, patterns, and attitudes of our old life. He has made us alive, when we were dead, so that we can walk free with Him in a wonderful new way of living.

Have you some messy problems in your past? Are there old attitudes from your past life that caused you trouble and vexation; are there influences in you past life that have caught you in a negative psychological chain reaction? Then remember you are a new creation if Christ has become your life, and the old things need not hold you anymore: or control you anymore. You are a new person; walk free from the old habits and disadvantages, hurts, and sins, of the past. He has empowered you for a new life. Ignore your old bandages, walk away from them, leave them buried and covered in the tomb.

A Prayer

Lord Jesus, I have received your life into my heart and now I want to be controlled by that new life and not by my old ways. Thanks to you, I am a new creation, my old life has no more power over me. With you I walk free from every sin, habit pattern, regret, and bondage from my old life to a new life of freedom as I cleave to you. Thank you that I am free. Amen.

Chapter Twenty

MOUNT OF OLIVES & THE GOLDEN GATE

From the vantage point of the Mount of Olives one can look over the Old City of Jerusalem. Jesus came here frequently to pray. From here He rode into Jerusalem on a colt, entering through the Eastern Gate in triumph. Jesus' coronation procession has been interrupted, as it were, by His crucifixion, but He has been crowned in heaven and in the hearts of those who believe in Him. Soon He will return arid His feet will touch this Mount of Olives once again. With His overcomers King Jesus will establish His rule throughout this earth.

"So when they had come together, they asked him, 'Lord, will you at this time restore the kingdom to Israel?' He said to them, 'It is not for you to know the times or seasons which the Father has fixed by his own authority. But you shall receive power when the Holy Spirit has come upon you; and you shall be my witnesses in Jerusalem and in all Judea and Samaria and to the end of the earth.' And when he had said this, as they were looking on, He was lifted up, and a

cloud took Him out of their sight. And while they were gazing into heaven as He went, behold, two men stood by them in white robes, and said, 'Men of Galilee, why do you stand looking into heaven? This Jesus, who was taken up from you into heaven, will come in the same way as you saw Him go into heaven.' Then they returned to Jerusalem from the Mount called Olivet which is near Jerusalem." (Acts 1:6-12)

"Behold, a day of the Lord is coming, when the spoil taken from you will be divided in the midst of you. For I will gather all the nations against Jerusalem to battle, and the city shall be taken and the houses plundered and the women ravished; half of the city shall go into exile, but the rest of the people shall not be cut off from the city. Then the Lord will go forth and fight against those nations as when He fights on a day of battle. On that day his feet shall stand on the mount of olives which lies before Jerusalem on the east; and the Mount of Olives shall be split in two from east to west by a very wide valley.

On that day living waters shall flow out from Jerusalem, half of them to the eastern sea and half of them to the western sea; it shall continue in summer as in winter. And the Lord will become king over all the earth; on that day the Lord will be one and his name one." (Zech 14:1-4;8-9)

Jesus the Messiah will come to take His place as king of the Jews and eternal heir to the throne of

David in Jerusalem. He shall rule on earth and administer justice to the nations. Jesus is a king who has come to bring a kingdom, and will return to complete that kingdom.

He came first in humility as the Lamb of God to take away our sins, He will return as the King of kings and the Lord of lords. He will return as the "Lion of Judah." The Jewish people for the most part missed the prophecies in the scripture which showed that it "was necessary that the Messiah should suffer" before He entered into His glory. Many Christians miss the prophecies which say that He will return in glory. Upon His triumphant return He will establish His glorious kingdom on this earth, and turn this world into the beautiful place of peace and fruitfulness that God intends it to be.

The apostle Peter pointed out, however, that Jesus "must be retained in heaven until the time of the restoration of all things." (Acts 3:21) Before our eyes today we can see the restoration of the Church and the restoration of Israel. The restoration of all things is nearly complete. Jesus is waiting until the Holy Spirit has completed His work of restoring Hispeople and transforming them (or at least a remnant of them) into a glorious Bride who will rule with Him over the nations on earth and be the new Jerusalem.

Jesus will not rule alone over the earth, He will rule with His saints from every tribe and tongue and people and nation. The Holy Spirit has been drawing out from the nations a people who will rule with Him. When His Bride has been prepared, and has prepared herself, He will return to rule on the throne of David. The ruling Messiah will be the head of a Body of tried and tested ones who have been matured in the same way as He was perfected in His days on earth.

"But when you see Jerusalem surrounded by armies, then know that its desolation has come near. Then let those who are in Judea flee to the mountains, and let those who are inside the city depart, and let not those who are out in the country enter it; for these are days of vengeance, to fulfill all that is written.

Alas for those who are with child and for those who give suck in those days! For great distress shall be upon the earth and wrath upon this people; they will fall by the edge of the sword, and be led captive among all nations; and Jerusalem will be trodden down by the Gentiles, until the times of the Gentiles are fulfilled. And there will be signs in sun and moon and stars, and upon the earth distress of nations in perplexity at the roaring of the sea and the waves, men fainting with fear and with foreboding of what is coming on the world; for the powers of the heavens will be shaken. And then they will see the Son of man coming in a cloud with power and great glory. Now when these things begin to take place, look up and raise your heads, because your redemption is drawing near." (Luke 21:20-24)

Jesus predicted the destruction of Jerusalem and the scattering of His own people. But He also predicted that their scattering would not be forever. He predicted that Jerusalem would come back to Jewish control.

We now know that His prophecies were 100% accurate. In 1967 Jerusalem came back to Jewish control Jesus' words indicate however, that the generation that sees the end of Gentile domination over Jerusalem will be the generation that experiences the full establishment of His kingdom on earth and His promised return to the Mount of Olives

The Sealed Gate

Today when we stand on the Mount of Olives we look across the Kidron valley to the Temple Mount area. The walls of Jerusalem circle the Old City and the temple area like a wreath. The walls have twelve gates built to allow traffic of people and supplies enter and leave the city. One of these gates, the Eastern Gate (The Golden Gate) faces East to the Mount of Olives.

The walls that surround the Old City of Jerusalem stretch for more than two miles. They were built in the days of Suleiman the Magnificent (1538-1541) on the ruins of walls dating from the days of Saladin who defeated the Crusaders, and on earlier walls that date back to the days of Herod the Great. In the days of the Second Temple the Golden Gate provided immediate access into the Temple area. It was through this gate that Jesus walked on the day He rode triumphantly from the Mount of Olives. He then entered the Temple and subsequently drove out the merchants.

In his vision, Ezekiel saw the Eastern Gate as it is today, sealed tightly shut. *"And he said to me, "This gate shall remain shut; it shall not be opened, and no one shall enter by it; for the LORD, the God of Israel, has entered by it; therefore it shall remain shut."* (Ezekiel 44:2) According to his vision the gate is to remain shut until Messiah Jesus enters it again. Knowing this prophecy the Moslems have sealed this gate to prevent the Jewish Messiah entering it. Unwittingly they have been fulfilling the very scripture that they have been trying to prevent.

Twice in this century plans have been made to open the gate, but each time (in 1917 and again in 1967) the plans have been interrupted by the events of war. Today the gate remains closed silently waiting for the moment the Messiah will return in glory and repeat His journey from the Mount of Olives, through the Golden Gate into the temple area. This time he will come not to be crucified to bear the sins of the people, but He will come with ten thousand of His saints (a cleansed temple without spot or wrinkle) and will bring the outer glorious Kingdom of Righteousness and Peace with Him.

The Golden gate, silent sentinel of the truth of prophecy and the hope of Israel waits for the Messiah to come. The hour of fulfillment is nearly here. The King has already brought His Kingdom with Him into the hearts of believers. When He returns He will bring the outer rule of God on earth. His kingdom is coming to earth.

Today there are millions of people who work and pray for world peace. Jesus taught us to pray for the coming of God's Kingdom. The day of world peace is coming. It will not come through the peace treaties and diplomatic maneuverings of the great political powers. It will come, as all the scriptures testify through the establishment of the throne of David in Jerusalem. When will this gate be opened? When will peace come to this earth? When will Jesus return in triumph? *"When the Lord shall build up Zion, he will appear in his glory."* (Psalm 102:16) The restoration of Israel and the restoration of the church is without doubt part of the building up of Zion. We can co-operate with this work, by helping and comforting the Jewish people in their mission to return and build up their homeland, and by working for the restoration of true Christianity.

A Prayer

Lord, give me a heart to understand the times in which we live in the perspective of your eternal plan. Hasten the day of your return and use me as a witness of your love and truth as we await it. Amen.

Chapter Twenty-One

The Upper Room
Passover & The Last Supper

Then came the day of Unleavened Bread, on which the Passover lamb had to be sacrificed. So Jesus sent Peter and John, saying, "Go and prepare the Passover for us, that we may eat it." They said to him, "Where will you have us prepare it?"

He said to them, "Behold, when you have entered the city, a man carrying a jar of water will meet you; follow him into the house which he enters, and tell the householder, 'The Teacher says to you, Where is the guest room, where I am to eat the Passover with my disciples?'

And he will show you a large upper room furnished; there make ready. And they went, and found it as he had told them; and they prepared the Passover. And when the hour came, he sat at table, and the apostles with him. And he said to them, "I have earnestly desired to eat this Passover with you before I suffer; for I tell you I shall not eat it until it is fulfilled in the kingdom of God."

And he took a cup, and when he had given thanks he said, "Take this, and divide it among

131

yourselves; for I tell you that from now on I shall not drink of the fruit of the vine until the kingdom of God comes. And he took bread, and when he had given thanks he broke it and gave it to them, saying, "This is my body which is given for you. Do this in remembrance of me." And likewise the cup after supper, saying, "This cup which is poured out for you is the new covenant in my blood. (Luke 22:7-20)

The location of this room was in the area of Upper Jerusalem where the Essenes stayed. In those days, women normally carried the water jars but among the Essene men carried water. The disciples were told that they would find a large upper room in the area where men carry water. This indicates the friendship that Jesus had with the Essene community. It is likely that John the Baptist had come from that community and that many of the first followers of Jesus were Essenes. The Essenes were Israelis who were opposed to the compromise between the Jewish leadership with Rome and with Herod. They had withdrawn their support from the corrupted religious leadership that emerged from this compromise. They yearned for the Messiah and the kingdom.

In this area of the city we can remember the amazing events of Jesus' Passover meal with His disciples. He came to be the eternal Passover Lamb whose blood was shed for the emancipation of the

Jewish people and all who would believe from the powers of darkness and oppression.

The first Passover brought emancipation from Egypt, but this Passover brings believers out from the house of bondage to sin and oppression and restores them to the blessings of God. The Passover was also a prophetic picture of the death of God's perfect lamb, Jesus, for the sins of the world and for our emancipation from spiritual bondage. Jesus fulfilled the feast of Passover, through His death.

As the Jewish people embrace their heritage through the annual Passover meal, believers in Jesus embrace the realities of this great redemption through taking bread and wine in remembrance of Him. By faith we take and eat, and *activate through remembrance* the blessings of forgiveness, reconciliation with God our Father and restoration to His provision and care.

"All we like sheep have gone astray; we have turned every one to his own way; BUT the LORD has laid on him the iniquity of us all. (Isaiah 53:6)

Though every human being has sinned and is bound by sin God laid on our Passover Lamb the sins of all of us. It remains for us to acknowledge our need of it and receive this forgiveness. *"He was despised and rejected by men; a man of sorrows, and acquainted with grief; and as one from whom men hide their faces he was despised, and we esteemed him not.*

Surely he has borne our griefs and carried our sorrows; yet we esteemed him stricken, smitten by God, and afflicted. But he was wounded for our transgressions, he was bruised for our iniquities; upon him was the chastisement that made us whole, and with his stripes we are healed." (Isaiah 53:3-5)

Jesus understood that His death was about to fulfill this prophecy of Isaiah. He saw that the Passover lamb anticipated the shedding of His blood. His death provides atonement and a Passover for all who want to pass from slavery to sin and oppression to freedom under the loving rule of God. Isaiah makes it clear that the Suffering Servant (YESHUA) not only takes the punishment and blame for the sins of the world but also takes upon Himself the sicknesses of the world through His stripes.

This New Covenant not only brings remission of sins but also gives us a new heart, which replaces the sinful side of our nature with the life of God's Spirit. *"A new heart I will give you, and a new spirit I will put within you; and I will take out of your flesh the heart of stone and give you a heart of flesh.*

" And I will put my spirit within you, and cause you to walk in my statutes and be careful to observe my ordinances." (Ezekiel 36: 26-27)

Jesus did not begin a new religion, but He inaugurated through His death a New Covenant through which all can be reconciled to God, filled with His life and restored to His blessing.

This New Covenant is not just a reform or a renewal of the Sinai covenant. Though foreseen by the prophets and rooted in the heritage and hope of Israel, it is something totally new. It brings to believers permanent atonement, and an impartation of the Life of the Spirit which the earlier covenants could not do. Jeremiah makes this clear.

"Behold, the days are coming, says the LORD, when I will make a new covenant with the house of Israel and the house of Judah, not like the covenant which I made with their fathers when I took them by the hand to bring them out of the land of Egypt, my covenant which they broke, though I was their husband, says the LORD. But this is the covenant which I will make with the house of Israel after those days, says the LORD: I will put my law within them, and I will write it upon their hearts; and I will be their God, and they shall be my people. (Jer. 31:31-33)

"But as it is, Christ has obtained a ministry which is as much more excellent than the old as the covenant he mediates is better, since it is enacted on better promises. For if that first covenant had been faultless, there would have been no occasion for a second. For he finds fault with them when he says: "The days will come, says the Lord, when I will

establish a new covenant with the house of Israel and with the house of Judah; ... In speaking of a new covenant he treats the first as obsolete. And what is becoming obsolete and growing old is ready to vanish away. (Heb 8: 6 - 8; 13)

With the New Covenant also comes a new commandment which simplifies and fulfills the moral commandments of earlier commandments.

" A new commandment I give to you, that you love one another; even as I have loved you, that you also love one another. By this all men will know that you are my disciples, if you have love for one another." (Luke 13:34-35)

The New Covenant not only provides atonement for our failure to love one another but also provides us with the love with which we can love one another. Through the gift of the Holy Spirit the law of love is written in our hearts, and God's love is poured into our hearts. The older covenant could only point to God's standards the new Covenant empowers us to live by the new commandment.

Here at the Upper Room Jesus also gave us the privilege of remembering and drawing from all these amazing benefits through Holy Communion. By taking bread and wine in solemn remembrance of what He has done for us we activate the benefits of the New Covenant in our lives.

Chapter Twenty-Two

THE GARDEN OF GETHSEMANE

"And they went to a place which was called Gethsemane, and He said to His disciples, 'Sit here while I pray.' And He took with Him Peter and James and John and began to be greatly distressed and troubled. And He said to them, 'My soul is very sorrowful, even to death; remain here and watch.' And going a little farther, He fell on the ground and prayed that if it were possible the hour might pass from Him. And he said, 'Abba, Father, all things are possible to thee; remove this cup from me; yet not what I will, but what thou wilt.' And He came and found them sleeping, and He said to Peter, 'Simon, are you asleep? Could you not watch one hour? Watch and pray that you may not enter into temptation; the spirit indeed is willing, but the flesh is weak.'"

"And immediately, while he was still speaking, Judas came." (Mark 14:32-38 & 43)

"Do not think that have come to bring peace on earth; I have not come to bring peace, but a sword. For I have come to set a man against his father, and a

daughter against her mother, and a daughter-in-law against her mother-in-Jaw; and a man's foes will be those of his own household. He who loves father or mother more than me is not worthy of mc; and he who loves son or daughter more than me is not worthy of me; and he who does not take his cross and follow mc is not worthy of mc. He who finds his life will lose it, and he who loses his life for my sake will find it." (Mt. 34-39)

Here in the Garden of Gethsemane the weight of the sin and sorrow of the world began to come upon Jesus our High Priest and Intercessor. He was about to take on Himself the sins of the world. Was it possible for Him to fulfill His mission without drinking the cup of Calvary? Knowing that it was not, He said, "Father, not my will but thine be done." He had not come to do His own will, to find self-fulfillment or to make a name for Himself or to seek glory from men, but to obey His Father, that God could fulfill His purposes through Him.

"He emptied Himself and became obedient unto death, even death on a cross. Therefore God has highly exalted Him and bestowed on Him the name which is above every name." (Phil. 2:8-9) Jesus was not a masochist. He did not enjoy or welcome suffering, but knowing that there was no other way through which He could fulfill His mission to be the eternal Lamb of God to take away the sins of the

world, He embraced the cross. At Gethsemane He had His final struggles with that voice which had consistently tried to turn Him back from taking His cross. *"Jesus for the joy that was set before Him, endured the cross despising the shame, and is seated at the right hand of the throne of God."*

No one will ever again have to endure Jesus' cross, but each of us have our personal cross which we are to take up each day. We encounter our cross when God's plan for our life cuts across our natural desires and wishes and limits us. The result of taking up our cross each day is that we are conformed into His likeness more and more and share more fully in His glory. We do not take up a cross which has not been presented to us by our Father. Only when we are sure that a task is truly God's destiny for us can we embrace it as our cross. We know that the consequence of our obedience will be glorious. God is not asking us to crucify ourselves or to stamp on our personalities and talents, but to obey Him and to do what He assigns us to do, knowing that this path is the path to glory. Obeying Him may result in the forfeiture of many of our own plans and ambitions, *("he who loves life most must lose it")* put us at odds with our family and friends but it will ultimately result in our entry into a more wonderful destiny.

Here at Gethsemane, we remember not only the great love the Father has for us in sending His Son to suffer humiliation, and the obedience of Jesus, but we are inspired to say "Yes Lord!" to the destiny and to the consequences of obedience to Him that all of us must be willing to endure.

At Gethsemanie we are reminded also to watch and pray that we may not enter into temptation. The voice of temptation is any voice or thought pattern which would divert us from God's highest purpose for our lives. It directs us to seek our will rather than His, comfort rather than obedience, to please people rather than God. Without a life of constant alertness and watchfulness and of continuous communion we will be unable to withstand these pressures.

A PRAYER

Behold I come to do Your will, to pursue Your plan for my life, even when it goes against the grain of my likes, preferences and the expectations of others. I have decided to follow You, Lord, even when following results in being misunderstood, unappreciated and obscured. I say, "Yes Lord, Yes Lord, Yes Lord with the help of your Spirit I will obey." Keep me alert and in prayer drawing from your strength and following Your course for my life.

Chapter Twenty-Three

CAIPHAS' HOUSE
(PETER HEARS THE COCK CROW)

"Then Jesus said to them,' All of you will be made to stumble because of Me this night, for it is written: 'I will strike the Shepherd and the sheep will be scattered.' But after I have been raised, I will go before you into Galilee."'

"But Peter said to Him,' Even if all are made to stumble, yet I will not be.' And Jesus said to him, 'Assuredly, I say to you that today, even this night, before the rooster crows twice, you will deny mc three times."'

"But he spoke more vehemently, 'If I have to die with You I will not deny You!' And they all said likewise." (Mark 14:27-31)

"Simon, Simon, behold Satan demanded to have you, that he might sift you like wheat, but I have prayed for you that your faith may not fail; and when you have turned again, strengthen your brethren." (Luke 22:31)

"And they led Jesus to the high priest; and all the chief priests and the elders and the scribes were

141

assembled. And Peter had followed at a distance right into the courtyard of the high priest; and he was sitting with guards, and warming himself at the fire. New the chief priests and the whole council sought testimony against Jesus to put Him to death; but they found none...

"And as Peter was below in the courtyard, one of the maids of the high priest came; and seeing Peter warming himself, she looked at him and said, 'You also were with the Nazarene, Jesus' But He denied it saying, 'I neither know nor understand what you mean.' And he went out into the gateway. And the maid saw him, and began again to say to bystanders, 'This man is one of them.' But again he denied it. And after a little while again the bystanders said to Peter, 'Certainly you are one of them; for you area Galilean.' But he began to invoke a curse on himself and to swear, 'I do not know this man of whom you speak.' And immediately the cock crowed a second time. And Peter remembered how Jesus had said to him, 'Before the cock crows twice, you will deny me three times.' And he broke down and wept." (Mark 14:53-55; 66-72)

Today we can stand in the ruins of the house and courtyard of the high priest Caiphas where this event took place. The church of Peter Gallicantu marks the spot where these dramatic events happened two thousand years ago This event is not really a past event for it is an event that will be replayed Out in the lives of all who follow Jesus 'AT A DISTANCE.'

Peter wept. He wept bitterly. He had so wanted to be a faithful follower of Jesus, and now he had failed. He had told Jesus that no matter what anyone else did, he would follow and obey to the end; and now he has failed. He has failed the One that he wanted to please the most.

Jesus knew that in the hour of testing Peter and the others would fail. He was not shocked, surprised or angry when they did. Had He not predicted it?

There is a kind of courage and uprightness that has its origin in the strength and will of man. Legends extol it. writers describe it and movies glorify it. Some of us may have more of these strengths than others. If we are well endowed with these human talents, we will tend to think ourselves better than others (in all humility of course!) and we will look with pity on those less noble souls who are not able to live as uprightly as us. We may even consider ourselves exemplary and dedicated followers of the Lord as Peter did. All of these strengths and virtues of noble and dedicated character are fine, but make no mistake about it they will surely fail us on the day you hear the cockcrow. Peter had given up everything to follow and obey Jesus but he still needed another conversion before he could be a real follower of His lord. Before he could strengthen others he would first have to make the painful discovery of the limits and *complete bankruptcy* of self-righteousness.

Have you come to the place of the cockcrow? When we hear the cockcrow we suddenly remember the words and standards of Jesus. In that moment of shattering humiliation we become aware of the weakness and inadequacy of our own selves apart from the strength of the Good Shepherd. Have circumstances in your life or something you have said or done caused you to hear the cockcrow? It is only when we discover the limits of our self-righteousness, even our strong disciplined self-will that we can begin to really follow Jesus and lean upon His strength. This failure instead of being a disaster can become the springboard for a greater and more noble life, as it did for Peter.

Peter was no different than the rest of us, no weaker than the other apostles of Jesus. They had all asserted their willingness to follow Him to the death, but what they were willing to do and what they were able to do were entirely different things. Within twenty-four hours of the cock crowing one of them had betrayed Him, one of them had denied Him and the rest had run away!

Hearing the cockcrow Peter remembered the word of Jesus, came to His senses and realized that he had denied the One he admired most. He wept bitterly not only at the realization of his failure but at the more painful realization that though he thought he was strong he was in fact as weak as any other man.

Peter failed; but his faith did not fail. On the day of the resurrection we see him running to the tomb to find Jesus. The difference between Peter and Judas lies in this, that one in the moment of failure ran TO Jesus and the other FROM Jesus. It is not our sins that damn us. It is where we run AFTER we sin that determines our destiny. Jesus showed Himself to His disciples and showed them that their sins were forgiven and then He imparted a new life into them. This new life was the Spirit of God who would never fail in the moment of pressure as long as He was drawn upon. Peter and the disciples were new men. Strengthened by the Holy Spirit, these same men who a few days earlier had been so weak, will endure insults, imprisonment, and even death rather than deny their Master.

There is no self-righteousness in the life of the true Christian. The real follower of Jesus knows the absolute inadequacy of self-will and good resolutions. He is aware that he has no strength of his own. He has, however, found an endless new source of strength. By faith he has received and is learning to draw from the strength of Another. He is not shocked by the weakness and failings of others. He understands them because he has come to the day of the cockcrow in his own life.

Our flesh (our noble characters, self-discipline and good intentions) will fail us as it failed Peter, but Jesus prays that our FAITH will not fail. Why does He pray this way? Why does He not pray that our flesh would not fail in the first place? He prays this way because He knows that the best and most honorable flesh will fail in the day of sifting. He also knows that faith that draws from the Lord's strength will survive and overcome.

"I will all the more gladly boast in my weakness that the power of God may rest upon me, for when lam weak them I am strong." (2 Corinthians 12:9)

"This is the victory that overcomes the world, our faith" (1 John 5:4)

Jesus did not come to make us strong but to connect even the weakest of us with His strength.

Now see Peter on the day of Pentecost and in the years that followed, boldly testifying before multitudes, before kings and rulers before religious inquisitors and finally submitting to death for his testimony to his Savior. How did this same Peter become a man of such strength? He had learned his lesson on the day the cock crowed to draw no more from his own strength but to draw only from the strength of Christ. It was no longer Peter's strength but Christ's strength in him.

Have you been converted from the strength of self to the strength of Christ? Have you come away from and totally renounced self-righteousness to draw by faith from the righteousness of God Himself? It is not enough to be converted to follow Jesus. There is a second conversion where we cease to serve Him in the power of our strength and will, and instead by faith draw all our strength and righteousness from Him alone. This is true repentance.

A Prayer

Lord, I accept Your call to the highest life of righteousness and love. I acknowledge not only my failure to live such a life, but also my radical inability to live such a life. I accept Your complete forgiveness of my failure in the past and now I choose to go the way of faith. From now on I will rely on Your strength and will draw on it completely for every situation. Fill me constantly with the strength, love, uprightness and courage that can come only from Your Holy Spirit.

Chapter Twenty-four

THE PRAETORIUM

"But Jesus gave no answer. Pilate therefore said to Him, 'You will not speak to me? Do you not know that I have power to release you, and power to crucify you?' Jesus answered him, 'You would have no power over me unless it had been given you from above; therefore he who delivered me to you has the greater sin.'

Upon this Pilate sought to release Him, but the Jews cried out, 'If you release this man you are not Caesar's friend; everyone who makes himself a king sets himself against Caesar.' When Pilate heard these words, he brought Jesus out and sat down on the judgment seat at a place called The Pavement, and in Hebrew, Gabbatha." (John 19:9-13)

"Then the soldiers of the governor took Jesus into the PRAETORIUM, and they gathered the whole battalion before Him. And they stripped Him and put a scarlet robe upon Him, and plaiting a crown of thorns they put it on His head, and put a reed in His right hand. And kneeling before Him they mocked Him saying, 'Hail, King of the Jews!' And they spat upon

Him, and took the reed and struck Him on the head. And when they had mocked Him, they stripped Him of the robe, and put His own clothes on Him and led Him away to crucify Him." (Mt. 27:27-32)

The Praetorium was part of Herod's palace and the residence of Pilate during his visits to Jerusalem. It is now known as David's Citadel and is at today's Jafffa Gate. In the days of Jesus The Roman Garrison was stationed in the Antonia Fortress, which overlooked the Temple Mount. Here Jesus was publicly tried and mocked as a false king and false prophet. Here Jesus stood; here He was mocked, spat upon and scourged. His kingdom was not of this world. He was *"like a lamb that is led to the slaughter and like a sheep that before its shearers is dumb."* He was bearing on Himself the unrighteousness of the world. His kingdom would put righteousness in the hearts of the unrighteous. It would first be established in men's hearts and then openly to the world.

He who is King of Kings submitted to the abuse and the mocking laughter of the Roman soldiers. He did not seek the praises of men, the honors of the world, but to please His Father.

"A disciple is not above his teacher nor a servant above his master; it is enough for the disciple to be like his teacher, and the servant like his master... And do not fear those who kill the body but cannot kill the soul ... He who loves father and mother more than

me is not worthy of me; and he who loves son or daughter more than me is not worthy of me; and HE who does not take his cross and follow me is not worthy of me he who finds his life will lose it, and he who loses his life for my sake will find it." (Mt. 10:24-25, 28, 37-39)

Here at the Praetorium, Jesus took up His cross, submitted to total rejection by the civil and religious authorities and began the slow walk across the foot bridge over the Kidron Valley to the Mount of Olives and Calvary.

'Jesus, ... for the joy that was set before Him, endured the cross despising the shame.'(Hebrews 12:2) His eyes were not so much on the cross as on the resurrection, which would result from the cross. The cross is never an end in itself, but a means to God's end, which is life.

At the Praetorium we are reminded that each one has his own cross to bear. No one ever again will have to bear Jesus' cross. It is finished. Though He has completed bearing His cross we have not completed bearing ours. To take up our cross is to gladly and willingly do what God asks assigns us to do, even when it is inconvenient unpleasant, and does not make us look good. When obedience to God runs contrary to our own self centered ambitions, or to the expectations of family and friends we experience the cost of the cross. God has a 'tailor-made' cross for each of us.

151

Should we refuse to carry it, His purpose for our lives will be frustrated. When we accept it His plan for our lives is advanced.

To accept ones cross is to accept that which God has given us to do even when it means derision, thanklessness, misunderstanding, being thought of as a failure and living in obscurity. Those who take up their cross each day with joy will experience abundance of resurrection in this life and in the age to come.

We do not passively submit to circumstances or to "Pilate" but to those assignments that have been given us from God.

A PRAYER

Lord, I can only say a humble thank you for the abuse that You endured for my sake. Teach me and equip me to obey as you obeyed; to follow the course the Father gives me without fear of the derision or rejection of men. Free me from pleasing man that I may please you and so be of real value not only to you but to my fellow man as well. Give me of your meekness Lord and of your courage. Amen.

Chapter Twenty-Five

THE HILL OF CALVARY — THE PLACE OF THE SKULL (See also appendix III)

"And when they came to the place which is called The Skull, there they crucified Him, and the criminals, one on the right and one on the left. And Jesus said, 'Father forgive them; for they know not what they do.'" (Luke 23:33-34)

Jesus' death as a criminal outcast was necessary and preordained. He was destined to bear on Himself the condemnation guilt, sin and sickness of the world. He was killed during the Jewish Passover, because like the lamb whose blood on the door posts had saved the ancient Israelites in Egypt from the avenging angel, His blood was covering the sins of the world. He was as John prophesied "The Lamb of God."

"He was despised and rejected by men; a man of sorrows, and acquainted with grief and a'; one from whom men hide their faces, He was despised and we esteemed Him not. Surely He has borne our griefs and carried our sorrows, yet we esteemed Him stricken, smitten by God, and afflicted. But he was wounded for our transgressions, he was bruised for our iniquities;

upon him was the chastisement that made us whole, and with His stripes we are healed. All we like sheep have gone astray; we have turned every one to his own way; and the Lord has laid on Him the iniquity of us all." (Isaiah 53:3-6)

Jesus' death on the cross illustrates the evil that man is capable of. His death was outside the walls of the city. His blood is on Jew and Gentile; for the Jewish people called for His execution but the Gentiles carried out the deed.

His death on the cross is no tragedy or accident, however. He is not a victim of unjust circumstances, He is fulfilling His mission. God has sent Him to take on Himself the curse of our sins, the condemnation of our sins. Yes, we have all gone astray, *"but the Lord has laid on Him the iniquity of us all."* Your iniquity and mine, and that of every Jew and Gentile has been laid on Him. God has paid for our sins. He has meted out on Jesus the penalty of our sins and failings. It remains for us to leave our sin and guilt and sickness at the foot of His cross., accept the forgiveness from God that Jesus has won, arid come boldly into God's love and care.

There are two sorts of people on the earth today: those whom God loves ... and those who **know** it. God loves us so much that He put every record of wrong that stood against us on His Son. Ii remains for us to lay down our heavy burden and accept it.

A Prayer

Father, I am not sorry but grateful that Jesus died on the cross. Thank You for sending Jesus to bear the penalty of my sin, to be my Passover Lamb. I am sorry for my sins, but I gladly accept that they have been paid for by Your own Son. Thank you Jesus for taking on Yourself the condemnation that I deserved. I lay down now my burden of sin and guilt. I let go to Your cross my Adam life, all the inheritances and selfish sowing of my natural self. I know that the axe is laid to the root. Now Father knowing that my sins have been paid for, I receive your forgiveness and receive your love. Fill me with your spirit and give me a new life today under Your care. Jesus, thank You for the price you paid for me. Guide my life. I turn away from the confusion of my own way and I choose now to obey Your way.

Chapter Twenty-six

THE RESURRECTION

"And Joseph took the body (of Jesus), and wrapped it in a clean linen shroud, and laid it in his own new tomb, which he had hewn in the rock, and he rolled a great stone to the door of the tomb, and departed." (Mark 27:59)

"And very early on the first day of the week they went to the tomb when the sun had risen. And they were saying to one another, 'Who will roll away the stone for us from the door of the tomb?' And looking up. they saw that the stone was rolled back; for it was very large. And entering the tomb, they saw a young man sitting on the right side, dressed in a white robe, and they were amazed. And he said to them, 'Do not be amazed; you seek Jesus of Nazareth, who was crucified. He has risen, he is not here; see the place where they laid him.'" (Mark 16:2-6)

"On the evening of that day, the first day of the week, the doors being shut where the disciples were,

for fear of the Jewish people, Jesus came and stood among them and said to them, 'Peace be with you.' When he had said this, he showed them his hands and his side. Then the disciples were glad when they saw the Lord. Jesus said to them again, 'Peace be with you. As the Father has sent me, even so I send you.' And when he had said this, he breathed on them and said to them, 'Receive the Holy Spirit. If you forgive the sins of any, they are forgiven; if you retain the sins of any, they are retained.'" (John 20:19-23)

"I have been crucified with Christ; it is no longer I who live, but Christ who lives in me; and the life I now live in the flesh I live by faith in the Son of God. I do not nullify the grace of God; for if justification were through the law, then Christ died to no purpose." (Galatians 2:20-21)

The wonderful thing about the tomb of Jesus is that there is nobody in it. HE IS NOT THERE. Jesus is alive today. There is a man on the throne of the universe! A man who loves me enough to die for me. He is here to talk to us today, *"Lo I am with you always, to the close of the age."* He has promised to never leave us or forsake us. This man is God in the form of man and more human than any one of us. He is like no other historical figure for He is still alive on earth able to be present to all of us everywhere, whenever we call on Him, while at the same time He represents us in heaven. He has overcome everything and lives to enable us to overcome also. Though He is hidden now to many, He is being revealed to millions in our day, and will soon appear publicly to all. Death could not hold Him.

Jesus died as the representative of all men. Just as we died spiritually when grandfather Adam died, and we lost our inheritance through his forfeiture of it, so too when Jesus died as the representative of the race of Adam He took our sin and condemnation. WHEN HE DIED, WE DIED. When Jesus rose, the firstborn from the dead He came bringing His peace with Him.

Pointing to the nail prints in His hands He was showing His disciples that their sins had been atoned for. Fallen man has been forgiven. Then He said to them, *"Receive the Holy Spirit"* and He breathed on them. They were infused with the Spirit of God, which entered their spirits. Jesus is imparting His spirit to those who will receive this new spirit. Those who have received the forgiveness He offers and the implant of the Spirit of God into their spirits can go into the world as Ie went into the world. They have "traded" in their Adam nature for a new Jesus nature. They can walk under the Lordship of Jesus and live in the care of the Father. The control of the world is broken from their lives and heaven is open to them spiritually.

We are not under trial with God anymore. We were judged, but Jesus has taken our judgment and transplanted His sinless nature into us. Christianity is not a "self-improvement course" but a redemption. He has forgiven us the sins and inadequacies of the "old nature" and given us a new love nature. Christ is *in* us as a spring of righteousness and love and peace and joy. We live now not from the imperfect resources of our old nature but we live from Him. We are no longer laboring at *improving* our old nature, we are replacing it with the nature of Jesus. Our personalities and bodies remain the same but we have a new spirit. *"A new heart I will give you, and a new spirit I will put within you, and cause you to walk in my statutes and be careful to observe my ordinances.'* (Ezek. 36:26)

Have your received forgiveness and the new spirit He offers?

Have you laid down your Adam nature and received the new nature? Have you learned to live from the life of the spirit He offers and come away from living from the energies of yourself? We He died, we died; and because He lives we live in the kingdom of God.

The church of the Holy Sepulcher is the traditional site of the resurrection of Jesus. It has been honored as such since the days of Empress Helena, of Constantine. Different sects have fought over this basilica for centuries. Since the 1700's it has been shared by five different denominations - Roman Catholic, Armenian Orthodox, Greek Orthodox, Armenian Orthodox, Syrian Orthodox and Abyssinian Coptic, each of which has its own section of the church.

Though it may be hard to feel spiritual here amidst the bustle of tourists and the fumes of candles and incense, there is an aura of history in this place for nearly 1500 years millions of people from the ends of the earth have thronged here on pilgrimage.

Though the archaeological credentials of this site are no good, The Garden Tomb exudes the atmosphere of the morning of the Resurrection. Here there are no buildings to obscure the tomb and one can recapture the wonder of the Resurrection in quiet prayer beneath the canopy of a tamarisk tree. (For a discussion of the real site of the crucifixion & resurrection see (Appendix III: the Mount Of Olives)

The important point to remember is that the body of Jesus is not to be found in any site in Jerusalem or any place else, for He has risen indeed!

A Prayer

Dear Jesus, I know that you are alive and have conquered death. I know that your blood has covered my sin. I receive that forgiveness for all the defects and sins of my past. I freely and fully forgive everyone that has ever harmed me, and everyone I disagree with. I lay down my old self and receive your spirit. And now I dedicate myself to live no longer as a slave of myself but to go into the world under your Leadership as you went into the world. Father I thank you that the blood of Jesus destroys every barrier between You and me that my sins and the sins of my ancestors all the way back to Adam had erected. I come home to you to live in your care as your son (or daughter). I live to obey you that your purposes for my life can be fulfilled, and that you can channel your love into the earth through me. Holy Spirit I receive you into my heart to be the source of love and life within me; fill me with your love for all and the strength to live uprightly.

Chapter Twenty-Seven

THE EMMAUS ROAD

"That very day two of them were going to a village named Emmaus about seven miles from Jerusalem, and talking with each other about all these things that had happened. While they were talking and discussing together, Jesus himself drew near and went with them. But their eyes were kept from recognizing him. And he said to them, 'What is this conversation which you are holding with each other as you walk?' And they stood still, looking sad. Then one of them, named Cleopas, answered him, 'Are you the only visitor to Jerusalem who does not know the things that have happened there in these days?" And he said to them, "What things?" And they said to him, "Concerning Jesus of Nazareth, who was a prophet mighty in deed and word before God and all the people, and how our chief priests and rulers delivered him up to be condemned to death and crucified him. But we had hoped that he was the one to redeem Israel..."

"And he said to them, '0 foolish men, and slow of heart to believe all that the prophets have spoken! Was it not necessary that the Christ (Messiah) should suffer these things and enter into his glory? And beginning with Moses and all the prophets, he interpreted to them in all the scriptures the things concerning himself."

"So they drew near to the village to which they were going. He appeared to be going further, but they constrained him saying, 'Stay with us, for it is toward evening and the day is now far spent.' So he went in to stay with them. When he was at table with them, he took the bread, and blessed and broke it, and gave it to them. And their eyes were opened and they recognized him: and he vanished out of their sight. Then they said to each other, 'Did not our hearts burn within us while he talked to us (in the road, while he opened to us the scriptures?' And they rose that same hour and returned to Jerusalem, and they found the eleven there.' (Luke: 13-21; 25-33).

Since at least the clays of Moses, Israel has awaited a Messiah. What hopes were pinned on Jesus of Nazareth -"a prophet mighty in deed and word before God and all the people.' Thousands had hoped that He was "the one to redeem Israel", that He was the long awaited Messiah.

Jesus' disciples are sad and despondent as they walk the miles from Jerusalem to Emmaus. Their hopes are gone, because Jesus, whom they hoped was the Messiah, has been killed and Israel remains undelivered. Then Jesus (in disguise) walks up to them, and begins to explain to them the scriptures concerning the Messiah. He explains to them how all the prophets had foretold that the Messiah would first suffer before He would reign in triumph and in glory.

No doubt, He pointed out the them that as far back as the garden of Eden, God had promised that one of His seed would crush the head of Satan and in the process be bruised by Him (Genesis 3:15)' Perhaps He showed them how an animal had to die that Adam and Eve could be clothed (Genesis 3:21); how a ram had to be killed so that Isaac and his subsequent progeny could live. (Every descendant of Isaac owes his existence today to the death of that ram.) (Genesis 22.)

He showed them that the Passover Lamb, the Yom Kippur scapegoat and sacrificial lamb, and the daily sacrifices were given to keep before the people the fact that sin could only be expiated by the shedding of blood. "The wages of sin is death" and either we must pay for our own sins by our own death or something or someone has to die in our place. Jesus must have explained to the disciples on the road how Isaiah had predicted that God would send His servant (His Messiah) to suffer for the sins of the people and to bear their iniquities. Perhaps He explained to them that for a man to bear the sins of the people that man would have to be without sin. This would require a man without the sinful inheritance of the rest of the descendants of Adam. Jesus must have shared with them that God had sent His Messiah, a pure Son of God, to pay the spiritual, debts of all and then to be the ruling King of Glory. He surely told them how Boaz became the kinsman redeemer of Ruth, and how this illustrates that God has sent the Messiah to redeem His kinsmen who could not redeem themselves. (Book of Ruth)

Perhaps He reminded them that Moses had promised a prophet who would come after Him who would be greater than he: *"The Lord God will raise up for you a prophet from your brethren as he raised me up. You shall listen to him in whatever he tells you."* (Deuteronomy 18:15) (Isaiah 53) He may have recalled for them the promise given to David that his descendant would sit on the throne of Israel forever. David also predicted the death and resurrection of the Messiah "thou wilt not abandon my soul to Hades nor let the Holy One see corruption" (Psalm 16:10). The anointed one according to David would not remain to see corruption in the grave.

Jesus must have told these disciples, their hearts now burning within them, that Micah had predicted the birth of the Messiah in the city of Bethlehem (Micah

5:2). He probably explained the prophesies of Ezekiel and Jeremiah that the Messianic age would be preceded by a work of God to cleanse the hearts of the people so that they could walk in God's ways and not succumb to the sins that had destroyed them in the past. (Ezekiel 36 & 37, Jeremiah 31)

He surely would have told them that the Messiah had first to bear the sins of the people, as Isaiah had said, but that He would then dispense the Spirit of God to the people as Moses had dispensed the Law to them. He may have reminded them that the prophet Joel had prophesied that before the Kingdom of Israel could be fully restored, God would pour out His spirit on the Gentiles also.(Joel 2:28) Why is it necessary that the Gentiles receive the outpouring of the Holy Spirit as well? Firstly, because God has a peace plan for the whole world, and secondly, because if Israel is to live in peace and security the nations also must learn the ways of peace.

Did He share with them how the scriptures foretold His betrayal by one of His closest associates (Psalm 41:9) for thirty pieces of silver (Zechariah 11:12) that His demeanor would be humble and that He would not ride on a chariot but on a donkey (Zechariah 9:9)? Did He share with them from the great Messianic prophecies of Daniel which predicted that the Messiah would come within 490 years of a decree given to the exiles to restore and build

Jerusalem, and the Anointed one would be 'cut off' (killed) and that His death would be followed by a second destruction of the Temple and a second exile (desolation of the people)? (Daniel 9:24-27)

Now they saw, now they understood, God's Messianic peace plan as portrayed in the scriptures was different from what they had expected. Their hearts burned within them as Jesus explained the scriptures to them.

We may study the scriptures with the aid of dozens of commentaries and concordances and explanations of the real meaning of the Hebrew, Greek, and Aramaic words, but our spiritual understanding will be sealed until Jesus opens our eyes. Then what flood of light and insight will come to us!! Then our hearts will burn within us and the dry pages of the Bible will be electrified with life!!

One of the most tragic failures of Christianity is that Jesus has been proclaimed simply as Savior of the world, rather than as the Messiah of Israel, who was sent to restore the throne of David. He was to deliver Israel from its enemies, both within and without.

The Messianic Kingdom centered from the City of David would bring not only peace and prosperity to Israel but to all nations. Abraham had been promised that all the nations were to be blessed through his offspring, not only Israel; and Isaiah had prophesied that the Messianic age would be an age not only for

Israel but also for the entire world. If the nations were to live in peace with God and with Israel, they too would have to be cleansed of their sins. . The outpouring of the Holy Spirit as Joel predicted, would have to be on them also.

Christianity has presented the world with Jesus as its Savior while ignoring His identity as the Messiah of Israel. As we come towards the final days for the outer establishment of the Kingdom of God, both aspects of the identity and mission of Jesus will come into balance, and Jew and Gentile will be united in Him.

They had now arrived at the village of Emmaus. Their hearts were ringing as the scriptures had been turned from obscurity to light Revelation flooded their understanding. Jesus made as if to go on. They had still not recognized that it was he. They implored Him to stay, *"Stay with us Lord, for it is toward evening and the day is now spent."*

Has your life become laden with discouragement? Call out to Jesus to stay with you. He will not force Himself on you. He awaits our invitation to stay. Invite Him to stay and He will unfold to you the path of life. Often He comes to us in the disguise of ordinary events and conversations. Do not fail to recognize Him.

A Prayer

Dear Father, I thank you for your plan to bring peace on earth, by first putting it in the hearts of all who believe and then extending it to the world, Let your peace reign in my heart and use me in some way to advance your great peace plan for the world which begins with the Messiah of Israel. Lord Jesus stay with me and teach me your ways and lead me. Open my eyes to recognize you. Amen.

Chapter Twenty-eight

THE UPPER ROOM

"And on the first day of Unleavened Bread, when they sacrificed the Passover Lamb, His disciples said to Him, 'Where will you have us go and prepare for you to eat the Passover? 'And He sent two of his disciples and said to them, 'Go into the city and a man carrying a jar of water will meet you: follow him, and wherever he enters say to the householder, The teacher says, where is my guest room, where I am to eat the Passover with my disciples? And he will show you a LARGE UPPER ROOM furnished and ready; there prepare for us.' And the disciples set out and went to the city, and found it as He had told them, and they prepared the Passover ... And as they were eating, He took bread, and blessed, and broke it, and gave it to them, and said, 'Take; this is my body.' And He took a cup, and when He had given thanks He gave it to them, and they all drank it. And He said to them 'This is my blood of the new covenant, which is poured out for many. Truly, I say to you, I shall not drink again of the

fruit of the vine until that day when I drink it new in the kingdom of God.'" (Mark 14:13-16; 22-25)

"I do not pray for these only, but also for those who believe in me through their word, that they may all be one; even as thou Father, are in me, and I in thee, that they also may be in us, so that the world may believe that thou has sent me. The glory which thou has given me I have given to them, that they may be one even as we are one, I in them and thou in me, that they may become perfectly one so that the world may know that thou hast sent me and hast loved them even as thou hast loved me." (John 17:20-23)

"Then immediately after the ascension of Jesus they returned to Jerusalem from the mount called Olivet, which is near Jerusalem, a Sabbath day's journey away; and when they had entered, they went up to THE UPPER ROOM, where they were staying...

"When the day of Pentecost had come, they were all together in one place. And suddenly a sound came from heaven like a rush of a mighty wind, and it filled all the house where they were sitting. And there appeared to them tongues as of fire, distributed and resting on each of them. And they were all filled with the Holy Spirit and began to speak in other tongues, as the Spirit gave them utterance." (Acts 1:12-13; 2:1-4)

We were not there on the day of Pentecost when the disciples. 120 people in all, gathered together in one place to await the outpouring of the promised Holy Spirit. As they sat waiting, the Holy Spirit came UPON them to endue them with power to be His witnesses. The Holy Spirit had already come INTO them on the day that Jesus had risen from the dead to give them a new heart. Now He was coming to lead them into all truth and to give them the courage and ability to proclaim what Jesus had accomplished and the power to bring His kingdom to the ends of the earth.

Pentecost is the Jewish feast of Shavuot, or the Feast of Weeks. It is called "Pentecost" because it occurs fifty days after the feast of unleavened bread. (Pentekoste is the Greek word for fiftieth). On the feast of Pentecost each year the Jewish people commemorate the giving of the Law to Moses on Mount Sinai. We commemorate the giving of the Spirit to the church. The Holy Spirit is to be our guide and standard and He will bring to our remembrance the words of Jesus and Lead us into all truth. We are not only to commemorate the giving of the Spirit to the first disciples, however, we are to have our PERSONAL Pentecost, our personal experience of RECEIVING the Holy Spirit and being endued with power from on High. The Baptism in the Holy Spirit is for all who wish to be channels of the grace of God in their world today. "For the promise is to you and to your children and to all that are far off, every one whom the lord our God calls to him.' (Acts 2:39) Is He calling you to receive the promised Holy Spirit and to be endued with power from on High?

A Prayer

Dear Jesus, I thank you for being my Savior and Lord. Now I present myself to You in a new way. to be a channel of your love and blessing to the world. I want Your ministry to be continued on in the earth in some way through me, but I do not have the power for this. I realize that I cannot do this with my own ability, so I look to You and Your ability. I ask You now to baptize me mightily with the Holy Spirit and with power and to clothe me with "power from on High." Give me a Spirit of love and compassion, of power and might, of utterance and boldness of revelation and understanding and a Spirit of humility.

Holy Spirit come upon me now as my enabler. I yield my life to obey You, and for You to lead me in obedience to Jesus. I receive You now from the hands of Jesus with all your gifts and graces and I will speak in tongues as you give me the ability. Amen.

Chapter Twenty-Nine

JOPPA

"Now the word of the Lord came to Jonah, the son of Amittai, saying, 'Arise, go to Nineveh, that great city, and cry against it; for their wickedness has come up before me.' But Jonah rose to flee to Tarshish from the presence of the Lord. He went down to Joppa and found a ship going to Tarshish; so he paid the fare and went on board, to go with them to Tarshish away from the presence of the Lord." (Jonah 1:1-3)

"At Caesarea there was a man named Cornelius, a centurion of what was known as the Italian Cohort, a devout man who feared the Lord with all of his household, gave alms liberally to the people, and prayed constantly to God. About the ninth hour of the day he saw clearly in a vision an angel of God coming in and saying to him, 'Cornelius.' And he stared at him in terror, and said, 'What is it, Lord?' And he said to him, 'Your prayers and your alms have ascended as a memorial before God. And now send

men to Joppa and bring one Simon who is called Peter; he is lodging with Simon, a tanner, whose house is by the seaside.' When the angel who spoke to him had departed, he called two of his servants and a devout soldier from among those who waited en him, and having related everything to them, he sent them to Joppa.

The next day, as they were on their journey and coming near the city, Peter went up on the housetop to pray, about the sixth hour. And he became hungry and desired something to eat; but while they were preparing it, he fell into a trance and saw the heaven opened, and something descending, like a great sheet, let down by four corners upon the earth. In it were all kinds of animals and reptiles and birds of the air. And there came a voice to him, 'Rise, Peter; kill and eat.' But Peter said, 'No Lord: for I have never eaten anything that is common or unclean.' And the voice came to him again a second time, 'What God has cleansed, you must not call common.' This happened three times, and the thing was taken up at once to heaven." (Acts 10:1-16)

"These things I have spoken to you, while lam still with you. But the Counselor, the Holy Spirit, whom the Father will send in my name, he will teach you all things, and bring to your remembrance all that I have said to you." (John 14:25-26)

As we stand overlooking the ancient port of Joppa watching the waters of the blue Mediterranean break on this shore for the billionth time we are standing near the site of the house of Simon the tanner where Peter received the vision which would revolutionize the direction of the church. It was from here that the disgruntled, crusty prophet, Jonah, sought to escape God's directive to bring a word which would result in repentance and blessing to a wicked gentile people.

No doubt as Peter (who in this city had raised Dorcas from the dead) remained in Simon the tanner's house, his thoughts went out to those distant lands and islands beyond the horizon. Observing the seamen unloading their cargo from mysterious distant shorelines and shouting to one another in languages that he had never heard in Galilee, Peter must have remembered the words of the Master, "You shall be my witnesses in Judea, and in Samaria and even to the ends of the earth."

Then came the vision, and the invitation to go to the house of the Italian Centurion, Cornelius, and the subsequent pouring out of the Holy Spirit on these uncircumcised Gentiles. It was here at Joppa that the Holy Spirit altered his vision. God was blessing not only the Jews who turned to Him but was willing to pour His highest blessing on the Gentiles. He was showing Peter that He "shows no partiality but in every nation anyone who fears Him and does what is right is acceptable to Him."

Until this time, Peter and the rest of the church were all Jewish people. They believed that the blessing that they had received through the Messiah was only for Jewish people; now the Holy Spirit was showing this Jewish believer in Messiah Jesus that the blessings of the grace of God, the care of God, the righteousness of God, and the Kingdom of God were open to all men of every nation who would turn to Him in repentance and avail themselves of the grace that had been opened up for all men both Jew and Gentile, through the Jewish Messiah. The Gentiles would not have to become Jews to enjoy the blessings the Jewish Messiah has won for all. They would not have to be converted to anew religion to receive God's favor. They would simply have to put away false gods and renounce ungodliness and turn and receive the promised Holy Spirit and entrance into the Kingdom of God. In those days it went without saying that the Jew would not have to adopt a new religion or a new culture to receive the blessings his Messiah was bringing - forgiveness for all past transgressions, and the gift of the Spirit of God to reside within his heart.

We need to repent of turning Christianity into a Gentile religion. Over the centuries we have demanded that Jewish people who accepted their Messiah should renounce their jewishness. Just as Peter needed a revelation to see that Gentiles who accepted their Messiah did not have to become Jews, so too today the Holy Spirit is showing Gentile believers that Jewish people who accept the Messiah do not have to adopt Gentile ways.

The mission of Peter and His followers was not then either to create a new religion or to extend the Jewish religion to the Gentiles, but to proclaim and bring the blessings of the grace of God made available to all through the work of the Jewish Messiah, to all peoples everywhere regardless of their tribe or tongue or culture. Furthermore the Holy Spirit of God Himself would go before them as He had gone before the children of Israel in the wilderness to lead the way.

Jonah And Peter

Two men of destiny came to this port town, with a similar call, both with a vision from God, a call to deliver a word of repentance and blessing, not to their own people but to a Gentile people. It was probably over this last detail of the call that Jonah stumbled. Would God pour His blessings on a wicked Gentile people if they repented? He was to learn through much difficulty that God was more than willing to do so, as Peter was to learn later that God would bless any Gentile who feared Him and did what was right.

The blessing of the Gentile, though sometimes forgotten by the Jewish people in their preoccupation with their personal struggle has always been at the heart of their call. Had not God said to Abraham, 'In you ALL THE FAMILIES OF The EARTH shall be blessed.' It is not that God was rejecting the Jewish people in favor of the Gentiles but that He was extending the blessing of His grace to all. It is not a case of God choosing to bless Gentile rather than Jew, but that He has opened up blessings to the Gentiles as well as to Jewish people.

A Prayer

Lord may your blessings extend on all peoples and your kingdom be established to the ends of the earth. Loose us from all prejudice against people of different cultures and race.

Chapter Thirty

CAESAREA

The city of Caesarea was elevated to prominence in the days of Herod the Great. He named the city in honor of Caesar Augustus and built a temple, a theater, a deep sea harbor and palaces for himself and the Roman governor there. Caesarea became the center of Roman rule in the land, effectively the capital of the province.

At Caesarea, Cornelius, a Roman Centurion, became the first Gentile to receive the Holy Spirit. (Acts 10) God used this experience to show Peter and the early Christians that the blessing of the grace of God was to be extended to all peoples on the basis of faith and repentance.

It was at Caesarea too that Herod Agrippa (grandson of Herod the Great); was smitten by an angel after He had instigated persecution against the believers and had killed James,. He had just delivered an oration to which listeners responded, "The voice of a god, and not of a man!" Immediately an angel of the Lord smote him, because he did not give God the glory, and he was eaten by worms and died. (Acts 12:22-23)

The apostle Paul spent two years in prison at Caesarea under the Roman governors Festus and Felix. During this time of imprisonment Paul appealed to be tried in Rome and defended himself before King Herod Agrippa. Paul shared his conviction so forthrightly that Agrippa said to Paul, *'In a short time you think to make me a Christian,'* and Paul said, *'Whether short or long, I would to God that not only you but also all who hear me this day might become such as l am - except for these chains.'* (Acts 26:27- 29)

Caesarea speaks to us today of the clash that will exist to the end of this age between the kingdoms of this age and the Kingdom of God. There has always been either conflict or an uneasy alliance between these two. Those who obey God will always be seen as a threat to those who seek to exercise absolute control over the lives of men. The preaching of the Gospel and obedience to the God of Abraham, Isaac and Jacob will always be considered a threat to despotic government. The consequence will be two-fold: persecution, and the advancement of the purposes of God. Paul was to write:

"Who shall separate us from the love of Christ? Shall tribulation or distress, or persecution, or famine, or nakedness, or peril, or sword? As it is written 'For thy sake we are being killed all the day long; we are

regarded as sheep lobe slaughtered. No in all these things we are more than conquerors through Him who loved us. For I am sure that neither death, nor life, nor angels, nor principalities, nor things present, nor things to come, nor powers, nor height, nor depth nor anything else in all creation, will be able to separate us from the love of God in Christ Jesus our Lord."
(Romans 8:35-39)

A Prayer

Lord, I have noticed that neither you nor your greatest disciples ever really fitted in with man's systems. Enable me so to obey you so that I fit in with Your plan rather than the systems of men. I know that you will stand with me through every difficulty. May I, like Paul, give thanks in everything and rejoice always.

Chapter Thirty-One

THE TEMPLE MOUNT

"When they came to the place of which God had told him, Abraham built an altar there and laid the wood in order, and bound Isaac, his son, and laid him on the altar, upon the wood. Then Abraham put forth his hand, and took. the knife to slay his son. But the angel of the Lord called to him from heaven, and said, 'Abraham, Abraham.' And he said, 'Here I am.' He said, 'Do not lay your hand on the lad or do anything to him; for now that you fear God seeing that you have not withheld your son, your only son, from me.' And Abraham lifted up his eyes and looked, and behold, behind him was a ram, caught in a thicket by is horns; and Abraham went and took the ram, and offered it up as a burnt offering instead of his son. So Abraham called that place The Lord Will Provide; as it is said to this day. 'On the mount of the Lord it shall be provided.'" (Genesis 22:9-14)

"And God came that day to David, and said to him, 'Go up, rear an altar to the Lord on the threshing floor of Araunah the Jebusite. So David bought the threshing floor and the oxen for fifth shekels of silver. And David built there an altar to the Lord and offered burnt offerings and peace offerings. So the Lord heeded supplications for the land, and the plague was averted from the Israel." (2 Samuel 24:18, 24-25)

Abraham who came to Canaan from the area of Iraq came from a background of primitive religion where human sacrifices to idols were normal. He was willing to make the supreme sacrifice of his son to the one true God whom he had set himself to seek and to follow. There however, God showed Abraham that He was not requiring such sacrifices but that He himself would provide the sacrifice. In this there is a tremendous anticipation of the Lamb that God was to provide 2000 years later to take away the sins of the world. God does not demand sacrifice from us, except the sacrifice of obedience. He himself has provided the means where we can stand blameless in His presence and He Himself has paid for our sins. Here there we commemorate that God is our spiritual and material provider. He always will be.

Some 900 years later, David bought the site which was then owned by a Jebusite man by the name of Aruanah and used it as a threshing floor. David offered sacrifices there and made plans to have the temple built on that site. Solomon later constructed the Temple there.

The present magnificent building on the top of Mount Moriah protects the rock on which Abraham built an altar to sacrifice his son Isaac.

It was previously assumed that the innermost sanctuary of the Temple, the Holy of Holies, would have been exactly on the area that is covered by the Dome of the Rock today. More recent excavations, however, have shown that the Holy of Holies would have been slightly to the north of the present Mosque.

What is important for us to know is that this is the area where the Temple stood, and where God provided a ram to replace Isaac. Underneath the rock, which Aruanah had used as a threshing floor, there is a cave or cleft in the rock. When David sacrificed animals on Mount Moriah the blood dripped down on to the wheat stored below through a hole, which is in the middle of the rock. Water was used to clean the floor, and so water and blood drained down through the rock on the wheat that was hid in the cleft in the rock.

The rock is a parable in stone of our redemption. God has provided a Ram. He dies in our place and we go on to live because He died. We are "hid in the rock" like the wheat from Aruanah's threshing floor, covered with the blood of sacrifice.

The temple was built by Solomon around 900 B.C. It stood there as the center of Jewish life, and the symbol of God's presence with them until 586 B.C. when it was destroyed by the Babylonians. Seventy years later under the governorship of Zerubbabel, and with the exhortation of Ezra and Nehemiah it was rebuilt. The second temple was not nearly as glorious as the first. It lasted until 70 A.D. The years of the second temple were difficult years for the Jewish people. They endured the indignity of foreign occupation by the Greeks and the Romans.

Shortly before the birth of Jesus, Herod the Great restored the temple with the help of Roman money as part of a Roman strategy of conquering through appeasement. Jesus prophesied the destruction of this temple, because He saw that Herod had made the temple, which was meant to be a symbol of Jewish independence from the nations of the world and direct dependence on God, into a symbol of compromise.

The Abomination Of Desolation

The present ornate building, which stands on the Temple Mount was constructed by the Moslems in the 688 A.D. Inside the building in classical Arabic is inscribed, *"O you People of the Book, overstep not bounds in your religion, and of God speak only the truth. The Messiah, Jesus, son of Mary, is only an apostle of God, and his Word, which he conveyed unto*

Mary, and a Spirit proceeding from him. Believe therefore in God and his apostles, and say not Three. It will be better for you. God is only one God. Far be it from his glory that he should have a son."

We can now say definitively through the application of Bible chronology that this building is the "abomination of Desolation" referred to by Daniel and by Jesus. The abomination is not a future man but this building. This building makes it impossible for the temple to be rebuilt. And is dedicated to the lie that God has *no* son. *"Who is the liar but he who denies that Jesus is the Christ? This is the antichrist, he who denies the Father and the Son."* (1 John 2:22)

Bible teachers who are looking for some future dictator to sit in the Temple and make it desolate are totally missing the clear evidence that the antichrist spirit has been occupying the Temple and making it desolate for more than 1300 years!!

Many of the adherents of Islam are sincere, pious people and there is much to be admired in their zeal and dedication. However Islam is based on the greatest lie of all: that God has no son If God has no son then we are still in our sins, and if we are still in our sins we are still under the curse and cannot be blessed by God. the Moslem people will be blessed only as God liberates them from this lie and reveals Jesus who died for them to them.

"There are two phrases in Daniel the abomination of desolation" (Chapter 11) and the abomination that makes desolate (Chapter 9) The 'abomination' is something very bad and to make desolate is to 'make empty'. The abomination of Daniel 9 is the Roman army as described by Matthew 24:15 and Luke's paraphrase in Luke 21:20. the abomination of Daniel 12 is the Mosque. The Roman army made the city desolate, and the Mosque made the Temple desolate. The interpretation of the words of Daniel must be established by chronology and not by biased theology. God no doubt does not want the temple rebuilt, and so He allowed the Mosque to be located on that site! When Yeshua died, he said, "it is finished." No more sacrifice was necessary, and so God made the Temple reconstruction impossible by placing the Mosque on this site." (E.W. Faulstich 'Science & Chronology in Balance, p. 43)

The reason the prophecies of Daniel and Jesus are "sealed to the time of the end" (Daniel 12:4) is that only since we can factor in the bench mark years of 1948 and 1967 do Daniel's dates make sense.

"And from the time that the continual burnt offering is taken away, and the abomination that makes desolate is set up, there shall be a thousand two hundred and ninety days. Blessed is he who waits and comes to the thousand three hundred and thirty-five days." (Daniel 12: 11-12)

We now know that this is a prophecy of the establishment of the State of Israel what this means From 688 A.D. the year the Mosque the abomination was set up until 1948 is exactly 1335 years This prophecy predicts the exact date for the creation of the state of Israel.

*'Then I heard a holy one speaking; and another holy one said to the one that spoke, "For how long is the vision concerning the continual burnt offering, the transgression that makes desolate, and the giving over of the sanctuary and host to be trampled under foot?" And he said to him, "For **2300 evenings and mornings;** then the sanctuary shall be restored to its rightful state."'* (Daniel 8; 13) chapter 8 of Daniel is a prophecy about Alexander The Great. He conquered the Middle East including Israel in 334 In June 7th when he defeated Darius the King of the Medes. Exactly 2300 years later, to the day on June 7th 1967 Israel came back under Jewish control!

Jesus said when we se this take place *'look up for your redemption is near.'* (Luke 21:28)

We are the first generation EVER than can intelligently hope for the return of the Lord in our lifetime as He could not return until Jerusalem was back under Jewish control.

As abominable as the Dome of the Rock it stands as a silent sentinel to God's sovereignty over times, seasons, and history and to the accuracy of Bible chronology and prophecy.

Many interpreters of Bible prophecy look for an Antichrist to make a covenant with Israel and to rebuild the Temple. They speculate that he will then desecrate the temple and make it desolate. They fail to see that the temple has already been made desolate. Their theories, even though they are popular, are not really based on sound biblical Chronology

In the 12th century the Crusaders from western Europe captured it and converted it for use as a church. In 1187 the Moslems recaptured the site and it has remained in Moslem hands ever since then.

As we come to the temple mount our minds are filled with remembrance of all that has taken place on this site, from the day that God provided a ram from Abraham, to the days of David and Solomon, to the sad days of its destruction, to the days of its reconstruction, and second destruction. God will have a throne on the earth. Here we no~: only remember but we hope and wait in expectation for the Lord to complete the work of building His living temple. When the living temple is complete, the" head of the corner" can fit in His true place as King of kings and Lord of lords.

Remembering Abraham, we also remember that the path of faith and obedience goes frequently against the grain of our own understanding and preferences. If we surrender our way, He can be trusted to give us a more wonderful future and to fulfill His every promise. Let us move by faith like Abraham to look for that city whose builder and maker is God. As we do this we shall receive from God a new destiny and life, which is the product of His promises and not of our prowess.

A Prayer

Lord, thank You for the Lamb that You provided so that I do not have to die. Thank You for being my provider. I lay my life before you Lord to live on the path of surrender, obedience and Faith. Thank you that I am hid in the Rock of protection. Thank you Lord for this present day of restoration. Complete what you have begun in this nation, what you have begun in i me.

Chapter Thirty-Two

MASSADA

The desert fortress of Massada towers 1,400 feet above the Dead Sea. It was built by King Herod as a luxurious winter palace and place of refuge in the event of political upheaval.

It is not for King Herod that Massada is remembered, however, but for 960 Jewish nationalists who held out against the power of Rome in the years 72 and 73 A.D. Though hopelessly outnumbered and totally isolated from outside support they refused to surrender, until finally they choose to take their own lives rather that forfeit their ties to their country and be deported as slaves.

Massada today has become the symbol of Jewish links to their homeland and of their determination never again to be uprooted from it.

In the 1960's when Israeli archaeologists explored the ruins of Massada, they discovered in the ruins of the synagogue an ancient scroll of the Bible containing the 37th chapter of Ezekiel.

"The hand of the Lord was upon me, and he brought me out by the Spirit of the Lord, and set me down in the midst of the valley; it was full of bones. And he led me around among them; and behold there were very many upon the valley; and lo, they were very dry. And he said to me, 'Son of man can these bones live?' And I answered, 'O Lord God thou knowest.' Again he said to me, 'Prophesy to these bones, and say to them, O dry bones, hear the work of the Lord. Thus says the Lord to these bones: Behold I will cause breath to enter you and you shall live. And I will lay sinews upon you and cover you with skin, and put breath in you and you shall live; and you shall know that I am the Lord."

So I prophesied as I was commanded: and as I prophesied, there was a noise, and behold a rattling; and the bones came together, bone to its bone. And as I looked, there were sinews on them, and flesh had come upon them, and skin had covered them; but there was no breath in them. Then He said to me, 'Prophesy to the breath, prophesy, son of man, and say to the breath, Thus says the Lord God: Come from the four winds, O breath, and breathe upon these slain, that they may live.' So I prophesied as he commanded me, and the breath came into them, and they lived, and stood upon their feet, an exceedingly great host.

Then he said to me, 'Son of man, these bones are the whole house of Israel. Behold they say, Our bones are dried up, and our hope is lost; we are clean cut off. Therefore prophesy, and say to them, Thus says the Lord God: 'Behold, I will open your graves, and raise you from your graves, O My people; and I will bring you home into the land of Israel. And you shall know that I am the Lord, when I open your graves and raise you from your graves, O My people. And I will put my Spirit within you and you shall live, and I will place you in your own land; then you shall know that I the Lord, have spoken, and I have done it, says the Lord.'

'The word of the Lord came to me, "Son of Man, take a stick and write on it, 'for Judah, and the children of Israel associated with him; then take another stick and write upon it, 'For Joseph (the stick of Ephraim) and all the house of Israel associated with him and join them together into one stick, that they may become one in your hand."' (Ezekiel 37:1-16)

"My servant David shall be king over them; and they shall all have one shepherd." (Ezekiel 37:24)

At Massada we are reminded of the undying ties between the Jewish people and the land of Israel and of God's promise to restore them to their land. The present day gathering of the Jewish People to Israel is the fulfillment of this great prophesy of Ezekiel.

The condition of the people of Israel since 73 A.D. until 1948 is exactly the condition described by

197

Ezekiel. These years have been the "valley of dry bones" years of Israel, where they were victims of Roman brutality and of persecution in the European nations. These persecutions persisted in the Middle Ages and climaxed with the appalling holocaust in the 1940's when six million Jewish people were systematically slaughtered in Europe.

Ezekiel foresaw a resurrection of the people from all this death and saw them coming back to Israel from their "graves" in the nations of the world. Never again, according to the prophets will they be removed from the land.

The dry bones are coming together, the sinews are coming on the bones. God has said that when He draws them home He will put His Spirit within them, and save them from their backslidings. We believe that there shall soon be a great outpouring of the Holy Spirit on the people of Israel.

Parallel to the decline of the people of Israel the church too has been in a dry valley for the last 1900 years. It has not been totally dead or bereft of the spirit but far from the position of purity and spiritual power which it had in the first generation of its existence. We believe that just as the Jewish people are being gathered to Israel from their "valley of dry bones" so too is the church rising from its valley of spiritual decline.

The return of the people of Israel to their ancient homeland will prepare them to receive the rule of their Messiah. A parallel restoration will take place in the church which will prepare the "spotless Bride" to receive her returning king. As Teddy Kolleck former mayor of Jerusalem said, when addressing a Christian gathering in Jerusalem, "We will not be surprised if it is the same person."

The discovery of the scroll of Ezekiel 37 in the ruins at Massada and the coming alive of the nation of Israel is a signal to believers everywhere 1:0 be cleansed of their backslidings, filled with the Holy Spirit and prepared to receive their returning King.

The glorious coming of the Messiah, according to Ezekiel, will be preceded by the regathering of the Jews to the land of Israel. There they will be joined by the spirit filled Gentiles (the stick of Ephraim) and together they will form the restored Israel. In the end days, alert Christians will unite with awakened Jews in love and solidarity as "one stick" in the hands of the Lord.

A Prayer

Lord, we marvel that all the passing of years has not dimmed your eternal call to Israel. May the bones of Israel come together. May the breath of your life fill them. Holy Spirit, cause those whom you have brought back from many nations to be filled with your life. Strengthen your people throughout the world to serve you and to recognize your purposes in restoring Israel. May we believing Gentiles become one "stick" with the Jewish people in love and solidarity in Your hand. Amen.

Chapter Thirty-Three

THE WESTERN WALL

"When thy people Israel are defeated before the enemy because they have sinned against thee, if they turn again to thee and acknowledge thy name, and pray and make supplication to thee in this house; then hear thou in heaven, and forgive the sin of thy people Israel, and bring them again to the land which thou gayest to thy fathers...

Likewise when a foreigner who is not of thy people Israel comes from a far country for thy name's sake (for they shall hear of Thy great name, and Thy mighty outstretched arm), when he comes and prays towards this house, hear thou in heaven Thy dwelling place and do according to all for which the foreigner calls to Thee; in order that all the peoples of the earth. may know Thy name and fear Thee, as do Thy people Israel, and that they may know that this house, which I have built, is called Thy name. Let thy eyes be open to the supplications of Thy servant and to the supplication of Thy people Israel, giving ear to them whenever they call to thee." (1 Kings 8:34-35, 41-43, 52)

"But will God indeed dwell on the earth? Behold, heaven and the highest heaven cannot contain Thee; how much less this house which I have built. Yet have regard to the prayer of Thy servant and to his supplication,.., that Thy eyes might be open night and day toward this house, the place of which Thou hast said, 'My name shall be there, that Thou mayest hearken to the prayer which thy servant offers towards Thee in this place. and hearken Thou to the supplication of thy servant and of thy people Israel, when they pray towards this place; yea, hear Thou in heaven Thy dwelling place; and when Thou hearest, forgive." (1 Kings 8:27-30)

"Therefore brethren, since we have confidence to enter the sanctuary by the blood of Jesus, by the new and living way which He opened for us through the curtain, that is through His flesh, and since we have a great priest over the house of God, let us draw near with a tine heart in full assurance of faith, with our hearts sprinkled clean from an evil conscience and our bodies washed with pure water. Let us hold fast the confession of our hope without wavering, for He who promised is faithful." (Hebrews 10:19-24)

The Western Wall comprises remains of the enclosure walls built around the Temple in the days of King Herod. After the destruction of the Temple by the Romans in 70 A.D. the wall became the symbol of the lost glory of Israel. Through the long years of desolation (70 A.D. - 1967) the tiny remnant of Jews who remained would gather here and pray for the restoration of their people to their land and for the rebuilding of the temple. The wall came to be known as "The Wailing Wall" because of the lamenting note of their prayers.

Today the Western Wall is the symbol of the restoration of the city of Jerusalem to Jewish control.

Both Jew and foreigner gather to pray at this place. As they pray there towards the Temple site, they remember Solomon's prayer for all who prayed towards this place. Solomon knew that the Temple could not contain God. God lives in heaven and not in temples made with human hands. Yet he knew that the Temple was ordained to be the living symbol of their dependence on the One who sits and rules from the heavens. The Temple illustrated not only the centrality of the rule of God over the lives of the people but also their awareness of their need for forgiveness and reconciliation before they could approach this Holy God.

For nearly 2000 years the Jewish people have been left without their Temple, but God has not left them without a sacrifice to take away their sins. Forty years before the Temple was destroyed God made permanent provision for this when the great High Priest Jesus brought not the blood of bulls or goats but

His own blood to pay the wages of all of our sins. Access into the Heavenly Holy of Holies is now wide open to all who pray to God, because the blood of the eternal sacrifice has opened the way. It is absolutely Inconceivable that God would leave His people without a covering for their sins. The blood of the eternal Lamb is permanently on the Mercy seat of the Holy of Holies in Heaven pleading for forgiveness and Mercy for the sins of all Jews, Christians, Arabs, and all. How God longs for all to receive the forgiveness and intimate access to Him that has made available for us.

The Western Wall is back in the hands of God's ancient people. History is marching on. Paul writes: *"For if their rejection means the reconciliation of the world, what will their acceptance mean but life from the dead?"* (Romans 11:15)

The Jewish people are coming home not just to Jerusalem but also to a spiritual blessing that will surpass anything they have known in their history.

"I will take the people of Israel from the nations among which they have gone, and will gather them from all sides, and bring them to their own land, and I will make them one nation in the land ... My servant, David, shall be king over them ... and I will bless them and multiply them and will set my sanctuary in the midst of them for evermore. My dwelling place shall be with them; and I will be there God and they shall be

204

my people. Then the nations will know that I the Lord sanctify Israel, when my sanctuary is in the midst of them for evermore." (Ezekiel 37:21-22, 24,26-28)

A Prayer

Lord, I pray here at this place uniting myself with the ancient hopes and dreams of Israel. Forgive every sin and remove every veil, which may prevent both Jew and Gentile from recognizing your love and receiving your blessing. Amen.

Chapter Thirty-four

ARMAGEDDON - THE Hill OF MEGIDDO

"The sixth angel poured his bowl on the great river Euphrates, and its water dried up to prepare the way for the kings from the east. And I saw issuing from the mouth of the dragon and from the mouth of the beast and from the mouth of the false prophet, three foul spirits like frogs; for they are demonic spirits, performing signs, who go abroad to the kings of the whole world, to assemble them for battle on the great day of God the Almighty. (Lo, lam coming like a thief! Blessed is he who is awake, keeping his garments that he may not go naked and be seen exposed!) And they assembled them at the place which is called in Hebrew Armageddon.

The seventh angel poured his bowl into the air, and a loud voice came out of the temple from the throne, saying 'It is done.'" (Revelation: 16:12-17)

"Then the sixth angel blew his trumpet, and I heard a voice from the four horns of the go [den altar before God, saying to the sixth angel that had the trumpet. 'Release the four angels who are bound at the great river Euphrates.' So the four angels were released, who had been ready for that hour, the. day,

the month and the year, to kill a third of mankind. The number of the troops of the cavalry was twice ten thousand times ten thousand; I heard their number. And this was how I saw the horses in my vision; the riders wore breast plates the color of fire and sapphire, and of sulfur, and the heads of the horses were like lions' heads, and fire and smoke and sulfur issued from their mouths." (Revelation 9:13-18)

The Book of Revelations speaks of seven "bowls of wrath" that will be poured on the earth before the Kingdom of God and its King come to the earth in Glory. (Rev. 16) It also speaks of seven trumpets that are blown by angels before *"the mystery of God as He announced to his servants the prophets, should be fulfilled."*

There is a remarkable parallel between the events which follow the pouring of the bowls of wrath and the events which follow the blowing of the seven trumpets. So remarkable is this parallel that we can safely say that these two sets of events are the same.

Laying aside the volumes of "Bible fiction" (fiction with some vague basis in the Bible just as science fiction has some basis in speculative science) that have been written on the subject of the Book of Revelation and taught as doctrine, let us take a fresh look at this part of the Book of Revelation.

The seven plagues, which immediately precede the setting up of the kingdom of God on earth apparently, take place within a generation of the Jewish people's return to Jerusalem.

The sixth of these plagues is the Battle of Armageddon. It will be followed by the destruction of mystery Babylon, the entire political, religious and economic system that exists on the earth today insofar as it is built on the pride and ambition of man rather than obedience to God. This is the last trumpet, and it is at this point that the saints on earth will rise as their bodies are glorified and welcome Jesus back to this earth. They will rule with Him over the nations of the earth.

The world order (ruling systems) of this day is marked for destruction as the world order of Noah's day was doomed to destruction. That's the bad news! The good news is that after the destruction of the present world order, God's new order (the Kingdom of God) shall be established on the earth.

Those who follow the Lord will survive the destruction as Noah did and they will rule on the earth with their Savior and King. This earth is about to be made over. We are not those who despair about the future of the earth. We are filled with hope and optimism. After a brief period of difficult transition, the systems of this age which are build on greed, competitiveness and self-interest will be replaced by the kingdom of God, in which Jesus will be acknowledged as King and Lord. All systems of life will be based on service, love and wisdom. This is not fiction, this is fact, and we are living in the transition days right now!

The Battle of Armageddon is apparently a literal battle as well as a spiritual one. Armies will descend on Israel from east of the Euphrates River (modern Iraq) There they will be totally defeated. These armies are the armies of "the Beast" of the Book of Revelation. The Beast makes war on the Lamb and is defeated in Israel. (Rev. 16 &17).

"And I saw a beast rising out of the sea, with ten horns and seven heads, with ten diadems upon its horns and a blasphemous name upon its heads. And the beast that I saw was like a leopard, its feet were like a bear's, and its mouth was like a lion's mouth. And to it the dragon gave his power and his throne and great authority. One of its heads seemed to have a mortal wound, but its mortal wound was healed, and the whole earth followed the beast with wonder. Men worshiped the dragon, for he had given his authority to the beast, and they worshiped the beast, saying, "Who is like the beast, and who can fight against it?""

(Rev. 13:1-2) From Daniel we know that the leopard represents the Greek empire in the Middle East, (now Syria) the bear represents the empire of the Medes and the Persians (now Iran), and the lion represents Babylon. These are centers of the Islamic powers hostile to Israel today. These same nations will march on Israel where they will be defeated by the hand of the Almighty on the plains of Megiddo. [1]

After the defeat of the army of the Beast, Babylon is destroyed. At this time the followers of the Lamb are clothed in glory. ("changed in the twinkling of an eye") and join their triumphant returning King. This union, which takes place at the return of the Lord, is described as "the marriage supper of the Lamb." (Rev. 19:9) The Messiah and the Body of the Messiah will be completely united and will establish the Kingdom of God on earth in answer to the prayer that He has taught us to pray. Then God will pour out on the inhabitants of the land of Israel "a spirit of compassion and supplication, so that, when they look on Him who they have pierced, they shall mourn for Him as one mourns for an only child and weep bitterly over Him, as one weeps over a first-born." (Zec 12:10)

"And I will set my glory among the nations; and all the nations shall see my judgment which I have executed, and my hand which I have laid on them. The house of Israel shall know that I am the Lord their God from that day forward." From this time on 'the earth shall be filled with the knowledge of God as the waters cover the sea'(Is. 11:9)

Although we have every reason to believe that the Battle of Armageddon is a literal battle that will

---

[1] For more on this subject read "the False Prophet" by Ellis H. Skolfield

soon take place, we need to be aware that it is also symbolic of a battle that we wage daily against the forces that would cause us to build our lives on something less than the promises of God and the way of Christ. The Flood was a definite historical event that took place in the days of Noah. Noah, however, spent years preparing for this event by resisting the sins of his age and living a different kind of life. Today we battle daily against the ruling spirits of this age. As we fight this battle and overcome through obedience and faithful living we shall surely enjoy the victory which will ensue from the final overthrowing of these spirits and systems at the Battle of Armageddon and the subsequent fall of Babylon. Then 'the meek will inherit the earth' even as Noah did.

A Prayer

Make us victorious in our personal Armageddon battles. Keep us uncorrupted by the spirit of the Antichrist and the spirit of Babylon that is in the world today. May all our work and efforts have their source in you so that they can survive the coming shaking and be of lasting worth. Keep us free from the propaganda of false prophets and ideologies that fill the earth today so that we will always be followers of the Lamb, and never come against your people Israel.. Amen.

Chapter Thirty-Five

CONCLUSION

It is possible to travel the length and breadth of the land of Israel, and read over and over the account of the life and miracles of Jesus, without ever encountering the blessing and challenge of His life.

We can reflect on the miracles He did at Galilee, but what is important is that we meet Him today as the Healer of our lives and of our bodies.

We can recall the humiliation of Christ as we stand on the same pavement on which He stood, but if we fail to hear the call to follow Him and take up our own cross, we have simply heard the words but not the message. We have seen the places but have now caught the vision.

We can stand on the Hill of Calvary, but if we come away from there, still in our guilt and sin, of what benefit is it to us?

We can visit the Upper Room and remember there the miracle of Pentecost, but if we go from there without a zeal to be ambassadors for Christ arid without the power to communicate and bring His grace, we have missed the meaning.

We can see for ourselves that the Diaspora of the Jewish people has come to an end. However, unless we see with our inward eyes and hear with our inward ears the signal that is being given to us to arise and prepare ourselves to be part of the glorious company, which will usher in the King and His Kingdom on earth, we have not heard the message.

We can marvel at the scriptures that are being fulfilled today before our eyes in the land of Israel, but not get the point if we do not hear a call not only to stand in solidarity with the people of Israel, but also a call to bring blessings to all the peoples of the earth.

Our prayer for you is that, as you read these pages, (and if God permits, visit the land of Israel) a flame may be ignited within you - a vision of God's purposes in these days be imparted to you - and that you may be filled with a longing to have your life one in purpose and attitude with Jesus, the Messiah.

APPENDIX I

THE MOUNT OF OLIVES, THE MOUNT OF THE MESSIAH

Introduction

For centuries believers have debated over where exactly Jesus' resurrection and crucifixion took place. Now in the light of a greater understanding of Jewish traditions, closer scrutiny of the scriptures themselves, and archaeological research, the mystery is removed and we can confidently declare that Jesus was crucified and resurrected on the Mt. Of Olives

Evidence From Hebrews

Ezekiel 43:71 refers to an altar located east of the *Temple "without the sanctuary."* Here the important sacrifice. of the Red Heifer was performed. Where is this altar in relationship to the Temple? Jeremiah records that it was located near the southern summit of the Mount of Olives directly "east of the Temple," 'outside the camp' of Israel some 2000 cubits (about 1000 yards) east of the central part of the Temple. In the time of Jesus this was slightly down slope from the southern summit of the Mount of Olives in full view of the Temple from the west

Confirmation that Jesus was crucified near the summit of the Mount of Olives, about a half-mile east of the Temple Mount is found in the New Testament itself, in the Book of Hebrews. It states that the crucifixion occurred *"without the camp"* and *"without the gate"* of Israel (Hebrews 13:11-13).

These geographical references may mean little to us today, but to first century Jewish people in the Jerusalem area they could only mean one thing - Jesus was crucified on the Mount of Olives "without THE gate" and without THE camp." This refers to a special gate - the gate to the eastern region outside the city limits of Jerusalem. Golgotha was located at the southern summit of the Mount of Olives.

The Temple at Jerusalem was patterned after the Tabernacle of Moses, which was a portable Temple. The Book of Hebrews calls the Temple that Herod refurbished "the Tent." The Temple or Tent had three main sections and three altars. Most people only mention two altars, but the third is the most important when discussing Jesus' crucifixion.

Further east from the altar of burnt offering was the third section of the Temple called "the court of the Israelites". Outside the three main sections was a vast enclosure built by Herod called "The Court of the Gentiles". This court had an eastern wall with only ONE gate – a gate leading to the East from the Temple Mount over the Kidron Valley to the Mt of Olives. In the time of Jesus there was a double tiered arched bridge supporting roadway which led from the Eastern gate of the Temple to the top of the Mount of Olives It was built by the priests and was known as "the bridge of the red Heifer." It connected the Eastern gate to a sanctified road that led up to the third altar of the Temple, which was near the summit of the Mount of olives. It is this altar that is referred to in the Book of Hebrews and that was associated with the death of Jesus (Hebrews 13: 10-13) *"We have an altar from which those who serve the Tabernacle have no right to eat For the bodies of those beasts whose blood is brought into the sanctuary by the High Priest for sin; are burned outside the camp. Therefore Jesus also that He might sanctify the people with His own blood suffered outside the gate. Therefore let us go forth to meet Him, outside the camp bearing His reproach."*

We must recognize that this was a literal altar. The statement about 'the bodies of those beasts burnt outside the camp" is literal, referring to literal animals and the third altar is a literal altar of the Temple which was associated with the sin offerings. This altar near the summit was where the Red Heifer was killed and burnt and where special sin offerings were burnt to ashes in accordance with the Law of Moses. (Lev. 4:12)

Ezekiel 43:21 calls it the appointed place' located *"without the sanctuary"* and *"the outward sanctuary."* (Ezekiel 44) Unfortunately most Christians forget this altar. Recognizing its existence and importance plays a key role in identifying the place of Jesus' crucifixion. The sacrifices of this third altar are the prime ones mentioned in the Book of Hebrews. (Heb. 13:12-13)

Early Christians were familiar with this outside altar. They knew that the location' of these offerings was to be *"in a clean place" "outside the camp".* (Lv. 4:12). There was only one place outside Jerusalem in the time of Jesus where these offerings were burnt to ashes – the Mount of Olives

Jewish records from the period show the precise location of this 'clean place' where the third altar was situated is stated in the Book of Hebrews - east of the sanctuary i.e. on the Mount of Olives.

The Mount of Olives was the most sacred location outside the walls of Jerusalem, because it faced the Holy of Holies. From here one could look westward over the Eastern Wall of the Temple, directly into the sanctuary. The Eastern Wall was made lower than the other walls to allow full view into the sanctuary exterior, including the curtain hung in front of the Holy Place. The purification water of the ashes of the Red Heifer could only be obtained in Jerusalem opposite the eastern entrance of the Temple - the 'clean place' on top of the Mount of Olives.

Jesus was crucified on the Mount of Olives to purify not only the earth but also the heavens themselves near the spot where the purifications for Israel were ordained to take place. It was here that Jesus, the greatest of all sin offerings, was crucified for us.

The Garden Tomb & The Church 0f the Sepulcher Excluded

The Church of the Sepulcher, built by Helena the mother of Constantine, in the 4th century, and the Garden Tomb north of the Damascus Gate, have nothing to do with the rituals of the Old Covenant. The Eastern Gate and the Mount Olives, on the other hand, are closely associated with them in the Book of Hebrews.

During the Crusader period the rocks in the area just' north of the Damascus Gate were known as "Jeremiah's Grotto." It has no connection with the Old Temple types or ritual.

The hill outside the Garden Tomb With its cave holes does resemble a skull today and so was hailed as a possible site for Golgotha "The Place of The Skull" of the Bible. However in the time of Jesus these 'eye sockets' were not there. A traveler in 1610 drew detailed pictures of the area and his pictures show no skull-like formations. Over the past 20 years archaeologists have identified all the tombs around the Garden Tomb area, including the Garden Tomb itself, as being from the Iron Age i.e. 700 years before Jesus.

The Area of The Camp

In the first century the Jewish authorities established a 'camp area' surrounding the temple and the City of Jerusalem in the circular fashion that Moses ordained. The area of this circular camp, extended 2000 cubits (about 3000 feet) almost to, the summit of the Mount of Olives. Anything within that 2000 cubit circle would have been considered 'inside the camp' No executions could take place "inside the camp", (Numbers 15:35), and the scriptures specifically state that Jesus was executed "outside the camp." For a site to be considered as a possible site of Jesus' crucifixion it could not be within a 2000 cubit radius of the Holy of Holies. The summit of the Mount of Olives was outside this 2000 cubit radius.

Hebrews 13:11 says *"the bodies of those beasts whose blood is brought into the sanctuary by the High priest, for sin are ALL burned "without the camp."* Hebrews 13:12 says that Jesus also suffered *"without the gate".*

The camp area was a circle with a boundary that was 2000 cubits in radius from the inner Temple. It extended therefore beyond the walls of the City of

Jerusalem. This means that the area of the Garden Tomb and Church of the Sepulcher, though outside the *walls* of the city at this time of Jesus, were well INSIDE the *camp* and therefore could not possibly have been sites of execution, since Jesus was crucified outside the camp. (N.B. It was an important principle of Temple ritual that all 'unclean things', animal and human, had to be dealt with and disposed of to the east.)

Evidence In Roman Law

Roman Law often required that the place of execution was to be as close as possible to the scene of the crime or the scene the arrest. Since Jesus was arrested and executed by the Romans on the grounds that He claimed to be a king, the site of his 'crime' would be the most likely site of His crucifixion. The site where He permitted the crowd to hail Him as King was the Mount of Olives. Gethsemane, the site of His arrest was also on the Mount of Olives,. It would be logical therefore on the basis of their law for the Romans to crucify Jesus there.

On Palm Sunday *"as He drew near to Jerusalem, near Bethpage and Bethany on the Mount of Olives"* He let the people proclaim Him King of Israel and the world. (Mark 1 I: 1) Bethpage where He mounted the donkey was on the southern summit of the Mount of Olives (close to the altar of the sin

221

offering). This became the site of His 'crime' against Rome. When He was in Jerusalem, Jesus lived on the Mount of Olives. (Luke 21:37; 22:39, Jn. 18:2)

Golgotha

The word "Golgotha" is the Hebrew word for "skull". It is not identical in meaning to the English word. It does not necessarily mean the entire head, but "the top of the head", nor does it necessarily mean the head of a dead person. The Greek word 'krainion' is usually translated 'skull' but it too refers to the bony top of the head. The word 'golgolet' was also used as census term equivalent to the English idiom 'head count' or 'poll'. We do know that for Temple tax and other purposes head counts of pilgrims were made on the Mount Of Olives before they entered the Temple area. It is possible that the word "Golgotha" comes from these polls.

"Place of the skull" could mean either the summit of the mountain or a place where census were taken. It does no' imply a place with a skull-like configuration. In the early Christian era the top of the Mount of Olives Was known a the "rosh" or 'head' of the mountain

Evidence From Early Christianity

After the fall .of Jerusalem in 70 A.D. the summit of the Mount of olives was regarded as the headquarters of the early Christians. This was the case, until the time of Constantine. During the three and a half centuries before Constantine there is only one tradition of any 'holy place', which was esteemed by Christians – the Mount of Olives". In the Days of Constantine, the Church of the Sepulcher was a shrine to Venus!

Eusebius, the Bishop of Jerusalem, in thee days of Constantine, and a great historian, stated that Christians from all around came to visit the cave near the summit o£ .the olives and regarded it as the site of Jesus' resurrection. The focal point of pilgrims' interest in the early centuries was a cave just west of the skull (head) of the Mount. This cave was revered as Jesus' tomb. The tomb of Joseph of Aramathea had been a cave or grotto that had been enlarged and in this same area many of the early bishops of Jerusalem were buried.

Evidence in the Gospels

Perhaps the greatest proof that the Mount of Olives was the site of the crucifixion and resurrection of Jesus comes from the gospel accounts themselves.

"Jesus when He had cried out again with a loud voice, 'yielded up His Spirit. And behold the veil of the temple was torn in two from top to bottom: and the earth quaked and the rocks were split, and the graves

were opened; and many bodies of the saints who had fallen asleep were raised ... NOW when the centurion" and those who were with him, who were guarding Jesus, saw the earthquake AND the things that had happened, they feared greatly, saying, 'Truly this was the Son of God!'" (Matthew 27:51-54)

The scriptures plainly state that the centurion and the guards of Jesus saw Him die and at same time saw the veil of the Temple split in two. The only place from which one could see both – events was if one were standing on the Mount Of Olives This is virtually conclusive proof from the gospels themselves that the death of Jesus took place on the Mt Of olives.

During the Red Heifer and other purification sacrifices that took place on the Mount of Olives, the priests had to be able to overlook the Temple. According to Josephus the outer curtain in front of the Holy Place was about 82 feet high and 24 feet thick. It hung from a stone lintel and weighed about 30 tons or more! It was this curtain that was torn from top to bottom at the time of Jesus' death. From the Mount Of Olives the centurion and his party just like the priests With the Red Heifer sacrifices, had a clear view of what was taking place in the courts of the Temple.

Conclusion

The Mount Of Olives is the place of Jesus' end-time teaching, the place of His prayer for Jerusalem, the place where He was hailed as Messiah, the place of His arrest, the place of His crucifixion, the place of His resurrection, the place of His Great Commission, and promise of the Holy Spirit, the place of His Ascension, and the place to which He will return in glory!! It is no wonder it is called the Mount of Olives, the Mount of the anointing or the Mount of the Messiah. It echoes with the past and quivers with future promise.

The above is based on 'The Secrets Of Golgotha' by Dr. E.L. Martin. Available from Box 25000, Portland, Oregon 97225. Adapted with permission

Appendix II

THE RESTORATION OF ISRAEL IN PROPHECY

The return of the Jewish people to Israel and the restoration of the land that has taken place over the last hundred years is an event that has been foretold by the prophets of Israel from time immemorial. The number and detail of these prophecies are so overwhelming that not even the most skeptical reader can fail to be convinced that the hand of God is behind the return of the Jewish people to the land of Israel today. From Abraham to Zechariah the prophets foretold the events that are taking place today. Below are just some of the prophecies that predict the restoration of Israel and the return of the Jewish people to their land.

The return of Israel to their Promised Land is a testimony to the faithfulness of God to his covenant to Hs word and to His promises. If there is no God then the claim of Israel to the land is void. If God does not remember, or cannot fulfill His promise then He cannot be trusted. If He can change is mind about His promises then He is unreliable. But if He is real and if His word is reliable and His promises trustworthy then the people of Israel and their presence in the Land today is a testimony to the reality of God and His ability to govern the universe according to His word even the face of the resistance of nations.

*"'Abram passed through the land to the place of Shechem, as far as the terebrinth of Moreh. And the Canaanites were then in the land. Then the Lord appeared to Abram and said, "To your descendants I will give **this land**."* — Genesis 12:7

*"And I will establish My covenant between Me and your descendants after you. Also I give to you and your descendants after you the land in which you are a stranger, all the land of Canaan, as **an everlasting possession** and I will be their God."*

*"And Isaac went to Abimelech king of the Philistines in Gerar. Then the Lord appeared to him and said: "Do not go down to Egypt: dwell in the land of which I shall tell you. "Sojourn inn this land, and I will be with you and bless you, for **to you and your descendants I give all these lands and I will perform the oath, which I swore to Abraham your father**. And I will make your descendants multiply as the stars of heaven; I will give to your descendants all these lands; and in your seed all the nations of the earth shall be blessed."* - Genesis 26:1-4

"Then God appeared to Jacob again when he came from Padan Aram and blessed him. And God said to him, "Your name is Jacob; your name shall not be called Jacob anymore, but 'Israel' shall be your name." So He called his name 'Israel.' Also God said to him: "1 am God Almighty. Be fruitful and multiply; a nation and company of nations shall proceed from you, and kings shall come from your body. The land which I gave Abraham and Isaac I give to you: and to your descendants after you I give this land." – (Genesis 35:9-12)

"Then the Lord will scatter you among all peoples from one end of the earth to the other and among those nations you shall find no rest.." "Now it shall come to pass, when all these things come upon you, the blessing and the curse, which I have set before you, and you call them to mind among the nations where the Lord your God drives you, and you return to the Lord your God and obey His voice .. that the Lord your God will bring you back from captivity and have compassion on you and gather you again from all the nations where the Lord your God has scattered you. If any of you are driven out to the farthest parts of the earth under heavens, from there the Lord your God will gather you and from there He will bring you. Then the Lord your God will bring you to the land, which your fathers possessed, and you shall possess it. He will prosper you and multiply you more than your

fathers. And the Lord will circumcise your heart and the heart of your descendants to love the Lord your God with all your heart and with all your soul that you may live." — (Genesis 28:64-65; 30:1—6)

"It shall come to pass in that day that the Lord shall set His hand again the second time to recover the remnant of his people that are left from Assyria and Egypt, from Pathros and Cush, from Elam and Shinar, from Hamath and the islands of the sea. He will set up a banner for the nations, and will assemble the outcasts of Israel, and gather together the dispersed of Judah FROM THE FOUR CORNERS OF THE EARTH. Also the envy of Ephraim shall depart, and the adversaries of Judah shall be cut off Ephraim shall not envy Judah, and Judah shall not harass Ephraim. But they shall fly down upon the shoulder of the Philistines towards the west." (Isaiah 11:11-14)

(How accurately this describes 20th century and contemporary events!)

"But you, Israel, my servant, Jacob, whom I have chosen, the offspring of Abraham, my friend; you whom I took from the ends of the earth, and called from its farthest corners, saying to you, "You are my servant, I have chosen you and not cast you off"; fear not, for I am with you, be not dismayed, for I am your God; I will strengthen you, I will help you, I will uphold you with my victorious right hand. Behold, all who are incensed against you shall be put to shame

and confounded; those who strive against you shall be as nothing and shall perish. You shall seek those who contend with you, but you shall not find them; those who war against you shall be as nothing at all.
(Isaiah 41:8-12)

"Fear not for I am with you: I will bring your descendants from the east and gather you from the west: will say to the north, "Give them up!' And to the south, 'Do not keep them back!' Bring my sons from afar, and my daughters from the ends of the earth." –
(Isaiah 43:5-6)

"Lift up your eyes round about and see; they all gather, they come to you. As I live, says the LORD, you shall put them all on as an ornament, you shall bind them on as a bride does. "Surely your waste and your desolate places and your devastated land--surely now you will be too narrow for your inhabitants, and those who swallowed you up will be far away. The children born in the time of your bereavement will yet say in your ears: 'The place is too narrow for me; make room for me to dwell in.' Then you will say in your heart: 'Who has borne me these? I was bereaved and barren, exiled and put away, but who has brought up these? Behold, I was left alone; whence then have these come?'" Thus says the Lord GOD: "Behold, I will lift up my hand to the nations, and raise my signal to the peoples; and they shall bring your sons in their bosom, and your daughters shall be carried on their

shoulders. Kings shall be your foster fathers, and their queens your nursing mothers. With their faces to the ground they shall bow down to you, and lick the dust of your feet. Then you will know that I am the LORD; those who wait for me shall not be put to shame." (Isaiah 49: 18-23)

"Who are these that fly like a cloud, and like doves to their windows? For the coastlands shall wait for me, the ships of Tarshish first, to bring your sons from far, their silver and gold with them, for the name of the LORD your God, and for the Holy One of Israel, because he has glorified you. Foreigners shall build up your walls, and their kings shall minister to you; for in my wrath I smote you, but in my favor I have had mercy on you. Your gates shall be open continually; day and night they shall not be shut; that men may bring to you the wealth of the nations, with their kings led in procession. For the nation and kingdom that will not serve you shall perish; those nations shall be utterly laid waste.

The glory of Lebanon shall come to you, the cypress, the plane, and the pine, to beautify the place of my sanctuary; and I will make the place of my feet glorious.

"The sons of those who oppressed you shall come bending low to you; and all who despised you shall bow down at your feet; they shall call you the City of the LORD, the Zion of the Holy One of Israel.

Whereas you have been forsaken and hated, with no one passing through, I will make you majestic for ever, a joy from age to age. You shall suck the milk of nations, you shall suck the breast of kings; and you shall know that I, the LORD, am your Savior and your Redeemer, the Mighty One of Jacob." (Isa. 60:8-16)

'"Therefore behold the days are coming," says the Lord" that it shall no more be said, 'The Lord lives who brought up the children of Israel from the land of Egypt,' but 'The Lord lives who brought the children of Israel from the land of the north and from all the lands where he has driven them.' For I will bring them back into their land which I gave to their fathers. "Behold I will send for many fishermen", and they shall fish them; and afterward I will send for many hunters and they shall hunt them from every mountain and every hill and out of the holes of the rocks.'" - Jeremiah 16:14-16

(The final return of the Jewish people to their land is even more remarkable than their return from Egypt. This time they shall come from "the land of the north" and "all the lands". An exact prophecy of today's events. Their return will be preceded by exhortations ('fishers') and persecution ('hunters').

'Thus says the Lord God: "I will gather you from the peoples, assemble you from the countries where you have been scattered, and I will give you the land of Israel And they will go there, and will take

away all its detestable things and all its abominations from there. Then I will give them one heart, and I will put a new spirit within them, and take the stony heart out of their flesh, and give them a heart of flesh.." – (Ezekiel 11:17-19)

"And I will bring them out from the peoples, and gather them from the countries, and will bring them to their own land..." -(Ezekiel 34:13)

"I will bring back the captives of my people Israel; they shall build the waste cities and inhabit them; they shall plant vineyards and drink wine from them. I will plant them in their land, and no longer shall they be pulled up from the land have given them." - Amos 8:14-15

APPENDIX III

8 REASONS WHY EVERY CHRISTIAN
SHOULD STAND WITH ISRAEL

1. Because God Says He Will Bless Those Who Bless Them.

Genesis 12:3: *"I will bless them that bless thee and curse them that curse thee, and in thee shall all the nations of the earth be blessed."*

Isaiah 60:12: *'For the nation that will not serve you will perish; it will be utterly ruined.'*

2. Because We Owe Them A Debt For What We Have Received Through Them

Through Israel the promises and covenants were given. Through them came the law, the prophets and the Messiah Jesus, who has opened up access to God for all. Through the Jewish apostles the gospel first went to the nations. To the Israelites 'pertain the adoption, the glory, the covenants, the giving of the law, the service of God and the promises, of whom are the fathers and from whom, according to the flesh, Christ came, who is over all.' (Romans 9:4-5). *"For if the Gentiles have come to share in their spiritual blessings, they ought also be of service them in material to them in their material blessings."* (Rom. 15:27)

3. BECAUSE GOD'S GIFTS & CALL ON THEM HAVE NOT BEEN REVOKED

Romans 11:28*: 'As regards the gospel they are enemies of God for our sake; but as regards the election they are beloved for the sake of their forefathers. For the gifts and call of God are irrevocable.'*

Though most Jews have not yet responded to the gospel, this has not invalidated God's plan for them, which He will ultimately fulfill. The covenant with Abraham has not been replaced by the New Covenant, nor been set aside because of their failure to enter the New Covenant. Though the once for all sacrifice of Jesus has fulfilled and replaced the Temple sacrifices, the eternal covenant God made with Abraham, Isaac and Jacob and their descendants has NOT been set aside. "A hardening has come upon part of Israel, until the full number of the gentiles has come in, and so all Israel will be saved."(Rom 11:26)

4. Because God Has Promised To Bring Them Back To Their Land.

God has promised to turn, again to the Jewish people, to bring them back to their land and to cleanse them from unrighteousness.

"'I will restore the fortunes of My people Israel and they shall rebuild the ruined cities and inhabit them; l will plant them upon their land and they shall never again be plucked up out of the land which I have given them ' says the Lord your God.'" (Amos 9:14-15)"

"I will take the people of Israel from the nations among which they have gone, and will gather them from all sides and bring them to their own land; and I will make them one nation in the land, upon the mountains of Israel; and one king shall be king over them all." (Ezekiel 37:21-22)

The regathering of Israel is prophesized in Ezekiel, Isaiah, Deuteronomy, Amos, Hosea, Jeremiah, by Jesus in Luke 21:24, and by Paul in Romans 11. It is a key condition to the full flowering of the Messianic age. God promised Abraham and his descendants the land of Israel as an everlasting possession. He confirmed that promise with Isaac as recorded in Genesis 26:3-4 and again with Jacob in Genesis 35:12.

5. Because The Times Of The Gentiles Are Fulfilled

'Jerusalem will be trodden down underfoot by the Gentiles until the times of the Gentiles are fulfilled.' (Lk 21:24)

Jesus foresaw that the Roman Gentile armies would overthrow every vestige of Jewish rule in Jerusalem; but He also saw that that Gentile domination of Jerusalem would come to an end. In 70 AD Jerusalem fell to the Roman army.

In 1967 in the course of defending themselves against an attack from their Arab neighbors' the Israelis regained control of the entire City of Jerusalem for the first time since 70 A D. thus fulfilling this prophecy of Jesus. All believers in the words of Jesus should know that the ending of Gentile control of the city is God's plan. "When you see these things happen look up your redemption draws nigh." (Lk 21:28)

6 Because We. Are To "Comfort God's People"

In Isaiah, God speaks *'Comfort, comfort my people says your God. Speak tenderly to Jerusalem and cry to her that her warfare is ended, that her iniquity is pardoned that she has received from the Lord's hand double for all her sins'.* (Isaiah 40:1-2)

This is a call to Christians to comfort the Jewish people. Isaiah also envisions that the leaders of the nations would help the Jewish people and nurture them in their regathering. *Thus says the Lord God: "Behold, I will lift up my hand to the nations, and raise my signal to the peoples; and they shall bring your sons in their bosom, and your daughters shall be carried on their shoulders. Kings shall be your foster fathers and their queens your nursing mothers. With their faces to the ground they shall bow down to you and lick the dust off your feet. Then you will know that I am the*

Lord; those who wait for me shall not be put to shame." (Isa 49:22-23)

God says that the Gentiles will nurture the Jewish people and assist them in their reentry to their land. It is our divine mandate to help them for their own sakes and for the fulfillment of their unique call. Gentile believers must do more than observe what God is doing with the Jewish people...God is asking us to get involved in helping them!

7. Because We Need To Make Reparation For Anti-Semitic Teachings And Actions

Throughout the history of the Church, since the second century, Christian leaders have been guilty of the most vicious anti-Semitic remarks. These remarks have provided the basis for despots throughout the centuries to this day to ridicule, discriminate, and even kill the Jewish people. Often those who claimed to be followers of the Messiah (Rescuer of Israel, and the One who has taught us how to love and forgive) have perpetrated these actions. Can we blame the Jews for so often resisting a Messiah whose followers were anti-Semitic? In justice as well as in charity we need to make reparation for the tragic record of Christianity (both in its Catholic & in its Protestant forms) in its dealings with the Jewish people. We who should have been their nurturers; have so often been their enemies and tormentors. The spirit of anti-Semitism did not begin or end with Adolph Hitler but can find a landing ground on Christians who have not been awakened to their responsibility towards Israel

The heretical teaching that the Church has replaced Israel has been taught since the second century. This teaching is faithful neither to the Old Testament nor New Testament Scriptures. Though most nations and churches denounce anti-Semitism today, anti-Zionism is still widely acceptable. It is the new anti-Semitism. Opposition to Israel's right to fulfill their God given destiny in the land of promise is the most dangerous form of anti-Semitism today.

8. Because God Is Working With Them To Work Out His Plan For World Peace

Romans 11:15: *'For if their rejection means the reconciliation of the world, what will their acceptance mean but life from the dead?'*

The Messiah is coming back to Israel to be reconciled with His own people. He will reign from there with His overcoming saints *'from every tribe and tongue and people and nation'* over all the nations.' (Rev. 7:9; 11:15)

Isaiah 2:3 *'For out of Zion shall go forth the law and the word of the Lord from Jerusalem. He shall judge between the nations, and shall decide for many peoples: and they shall beat their swords into plowshares and their spears into pruning hooks;*

nation shall not lift up sword against nation, neither shall they learn war any more.'

World peace is coming. The fullness of the Messianic age is coming. But first there will be the destruction of all systems and kingdoms that ignore God's Messianic plan.

• If you want world peace. Pray and help the Jewish people;

• If you want to see the Church restored, pray for and help the Jewish people:

• If you want to see the Messiah return, pray for the restoration of Israel.

• If you want to see your nation and all the nations including the Arab nations) blessed, pray and work for it to stand with Israel and the Jewish people, and resist anti-Semitism.

• If you want your own life to be blessed, help and bless the Jewish people

• If you want your life to prosper, pray for the peace of Jerusalem.

APPENDIX IV

7 PRACTICAL THINGS BELIEVERS CAN DO TO HELP ISRAEL

1.   Study and understand what the Bible has to say about God's plan for Israel & the Jewish people.

2.   Pray for the peace of Jerusalem and for God's purposes for the Jewish people. "Pray for the peace of Jerusalem. They shall prosper that love you" (Psalm 122.6).

3.   Teach your church to stand with Israel. Organize a pro Israel event or seminar in your church or city each year to encourage biblical solidarity with God's plan for the Jewish people and Israel. This will bring a blessing on your church and city.

4.   Support (financially and otherwise) Christian agencies that help the Jewish people return to Israel and settle in their land. E.g. "The International Christian Embassy, Jerusalem".

5.   Share the Messiah with the Jewish people in the context of their own faith, destiny, and scriptures.

6.   Refuse to support anti-Semitic sentiments in public and social life. Where appropriate speak out as the Spirit leads in wise and loving ways e.g. notify politicians and/or media of your views.

7.   Visit Israel if possible. This is a practical way to learn about the people and support them and their economy. "Walk about Zion and go all around her. Count her towers mark well her bulwarks. Consider her palaces that you may tell it to the generations following." (Psalm 48:13)

In this time of international travel should we not all consider making Jerusalem our destination of choice?

SUMMARY OF THE HISTORY OF ISRAEL

2050 - 1760 B.C. Patriarchal Period (Abraham, Isaac & Jacob)

1760 - 1460 B.C. Israelites In Egypt

1460 B. C. Exodus

1420 - 1030 B.C. The Period of the Judges

1030 - 928 B.C. The Reigns of Saul, David & Solomon

931- 586 B.C. Period of Divided Monarchies of Israel and Judah. (In 722 Israel fell to the Assyrians; in 586 Judah fell to the Babylonians)

548 B.C. Cyrus Permits Jews to Return to Jerusalem

514 B.C. Temple Rebuilt Under Governor Zerubabel

432 B.C. Malachi, the Last of the Prophetic Writings is written

334 - 160 B.C. Greeks Rule over Israel 7 Middle east following conquest By Alexander the Great

300-198 B.C. Egyptian Greeks in Possession of Israel

198 -143 B.C. Seleucid Greeks (Syrian Greeks) Rule Israel

143 - 63 B.C. The Hasmoneans (Macabees) Overthrow Greeks r

63 B.C. Romans, under Pompey subdue Israel
28 A.D. Jesus is Crucified & Resurrected City of Jerusalem

70 A.D. City of Jerusalem & temple destroyed By Romans & Jewish People Scattered

72 A.D. Massada is Taken by The Romans

ca. 340 – 640 Romans Byzantine Empire Dominates Palestine

640 – 1099 Moslem Arabs Conquer & Control Israel

1099 – 1187 European Crusaders Conquer & Control Israel

1250 – 1517 Mamelukes (Egyptian Moslems) Rule Israel

1517 – 1917 Ottoman Turks Rule Israel

1917 Turkish Empire Collapses & British Under General Allenby Take
Israel. Balfour Declaration Permits Jewish Immigration To Entire Land

1922   League of Nations Gives Britain A Mandate to Supervise the
Land of Israel

1939 – 1945 World War II, (6,000,000 Jews Killed in Europe)

1948 British Withdraw & U.N. Approves Creation of the State of Israel

1967 Jerusalem Regained by State of Israel in Six-Day War
(exactly 2300 years to the day from when Alexander conquered the
Middle East. (See Daniel 8)the

1973 Yom Kippur War (Syria & Egypt Attack Israel)

1979 Camp David Peace Treaty Between Israel & Egypt

??? Confederacy Of Mid Eastern nations come against Israel and are
defeated at Armageddon.

???? Jesus returns in triumph to Mount Of Olives and
establishes world wide rule of Peace, Love & Joy!!

SHORT BIBLIOGRAPHY

Mitchell G. Bard *Myths And Facts - A Guide To The Arab Israel Conflict* American Israel Co-Operative Enterprise, Maryland 2002

Michael L Brown *Our Hands Are Stained With Blood* Destiny Image Shippensburg Pa 1992

Ken Burnett *Why Pray For Israel Pray For Israel*, U.K.

David P. Ebaugh *Key To Revelation* David Ebaugh Bible School Harrisburg Pa 1

E.W. Faulstich *Science & Chronology in Balance*, Chronology Books, Spencer IA 2001

Paul Johnston *A History Of The Jews* Harper & Row Publisher New York 1987

Hugh Kitson *Jerusalem The Covenant City* Hatikvah Publications Jerusalem 2000

Lance Lambert *The Uniqueness Of Israel* Kingsway Publications Eastbourne U.K. 1980

Ernest L. Martin *Secrets Of Golgotha* Ask Publications, Portland 1996

Paul & Nuala O'Higgins *The Four Great Covenants* Reconciliation Outreach Stuart Florida 1997

Paul & Nuala O'Higgins *Good News In Israel's Feasts* Reconciliation Outreach Stuart, Florida 2003

Bargil Pixner *The Paths Of The Messiah And The Holy Places Of The First Church,* Brunnen Publishing

Joan Peters *From Time Immemorial* Harper & Row NY 1985

Derek Prince *The Destiny Of Israel and The Church* Word Books Milton Keynes U.K. 1992

Basilea Schlink *Israel My Chosen People* Kanaan Publications, Darmstadt Germany

Ellis Skolefield *Sozo* Fish House Publications Ft. Meyers Florida

Ellis Skolefield *The False Prophet* Fish House Publications Ft. Meyers Florida 2001

Ruth Specter Lascelle *Jewish Faith And The New Testament* Bedrock Publishing Arlington WA 1998

Richard Wurmbrand *Christ On The Jewish Road* Living Sacrifice Book Company Bartlesville, OK 1970

PAUL & NUALA O'HIGGINS

Paul & Nuala O'Higgins are the directors of Reconciliation Outreach. They are natives of Ireland now living in Stuart, Florida. They travel extensively in an international and transdenominatinal ministry of teaching, reconciliation, healing and evangelism.

Paul holds a doctorate in Biblical theology and Nuala is a graduate in education from the University of London. They are the authors of several books.

To order books or contact write:
Paul & Nuala O'Higgins,
Reconciliation Outreach
P.O. Box 2778, Stuart, Florida 34995, USA
Tel. 772-283-6920

Books By Paul & Nuala O'Higgins
- Christianity Without Religion
- The Four Great Covenants
- In Israel Today With Jesus
- Good News In Israel's Feasts
- Have You Received The Holy Spirit?
- New Testament Believers & The Law

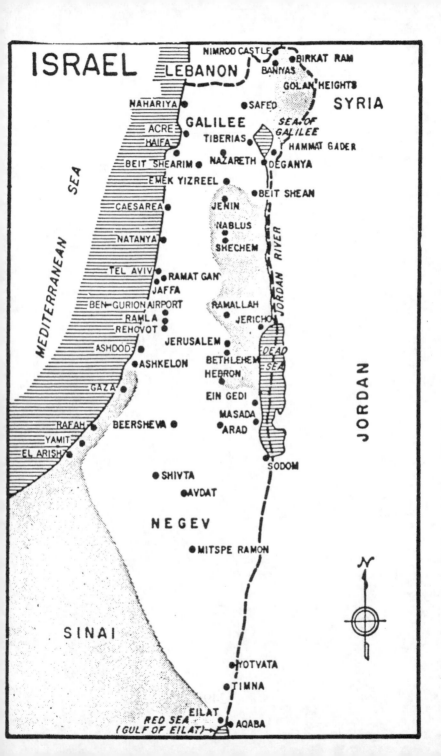